LANGUAGE ART: An Ideabook

Chandler Publications in
LANGUAGE ARTS EDUCATION

Lawrence W. Carrillo, Editor

Mary Yanaga George

LANGUAGE ART

An Ideabook

CHANDLER PUBLISHING COMPANY

An Intext Publisher · Scranton, Pennsylvania 18515

Some material included in this book is published and/or copyright as follows:

Arnold Arnold. *The Big Book of Tongue Twisters and Double Talk*. Copyright © 1964 by Random House, Inc. Reprinted by permission of Random House, Inc.

Esther Baskin and Leonard Baskin. *Creatures of Darkness*. Copyright © 1962 by Leonard and Esther Baskin. Reprinted by Permission of Atlantic, Little, Brown and Co.

Charles C. Bombaugh. *Oddities and Curiosities of Words and Literature*. Dover Publications, Inc., New York, 1961. Reprinted through permission of the publisher.

Dmitri Borgmann. *Language on Vacation*. Copyright © 1965 by Charles Scribner's Sons.

Elizabeth Coatsworth. Selection from "Swift Things Are Beautiful."Reprinted with permission of The Macmillan Company from *Poems* by Elizabeth Coatsworth. Copyright 1934 by The Macmillan Company; renewed 1962 by Elizabeth Coatsworth Benson.

E. E. Cummings. "in Just-". Copyright, 1923, 1951 by E. E. Cummings. Reprinted from his volume, *Poems 1923-1954* by permission of Harcourt, Brace & World, Inc.

Benjamin Franklin. "Be to thy parents . . ." from *The Autobiography of Benjamin Franklin*, ed. Leonard Labaree. Yale University Press, 1964. Reprinted by permission of Yale University Press.

Wallace Stevens. "Thirteen Ways of Looking at a Blackbird." Copyright 1923 and renewed 1951 by Wallace Stevens. Reprinted from *The Collected Poems of Wallace Stevens* by permission of Alfred A. Knopf, Inc.

Carolyn Wells. Limericks from *A Nonsense Anthology*. Published 1958 by Dover Publications, New York, 1958.

William Carlos Williams. "As the cat" from *Collected Earlier Poems*. Copyright 1938 by William Carlos Williams. Reprinted by permission of New Directions Publishing Corporation.

UNICEF. Three children's paintings from the 1965 UNICEF-Shankar Children's Art Engagement Calendar. Reprinted with the permission of UNICEF and Mr. K. Shankar Pillai.

To

"My Kids" at Sycamore School

and to

Laura Keiko and Matthew Bruce at home

CONTENTS

Preface   *xi*
Acknowledgments   *xiii*

Introduction   1

Part One: PROSE

1. The Constructed Situation   7
   Field Trips 7   : :   Animals 8   : :   Artifacts 9
2. Viewpoint   11
   Role Playing 11   : :   Biography 13   : :   Propaganda 15
   Hoaxes 16   : :   Heroes 18   : :   Television 20
3. Open-Ended Questions   22
   Sensory Questions 23   : :   Identity Questions: Objects 25
   Identity Questions: Self 26   : :   Sundry Questions 29

4. Serendipity   32

Alphabet Games 33 :: Tongue Twisters 33 :: Hidden Words 35 :: Word Play 37 :: Palindromes 41 Name Games: Acrostics 42 :: Name Games: Anagrams 44 Name Games: Election Predictions 44 :: The Current Scene 46 :: Equivoques 47 :: The Classroom Calendar 50

5. Skills   52

Spelling 53 :: Capitalization 54 :: Dictation 54 Summaries and Outlines 56 :: Timelines 56 :: Dictionaries 57 :: Bibliographies 58 :: Anthologies 58 :: Letters 61 :: Introductory Sentences 62 Quotation Marks–Dialogue 63 :: Quotation Marks– Puppets 63

Part Two: LITERATURE

6. Reading Aloud to Children   69

Background 69 :: Preparation 70 :: Expectations 71 :: Feedback: Discussions 72 :: Art Work 74 Written Work 74 :: Suggestions from Other Teachers 75

7. Developing a Sense of Form   76

The First Stage: Reading Aloud 76 :: The Second Stage: Following a Model 77 :: The Third Stage: Exploring Own Ideas 78

8. Developing Critical Judgment   80

A Word to the Wise 80 :: Constructive Assignments 83 Reading and Comprehension 86

Part Three: POETRY

9. Approach   91

10. Poets   94

[Frost, Sandburg, Williams, Cummings, Stevens]

11. Other Voices   104

[Belting, Cole, O'Neill, Merriam, Coatsworth]

12. Form   113

Haiku 113 :: Limericks 115

13. Senses   118

14. Books   123

Journals 123 :: Commonplace Books 126 ::

Bookbinding 127 : : Binding a Standard Book 127 : :
Binding a Japanese Accordion Book 133 : : Other Methods
of Bookbinding 137

Conclusion   138
Bibliography   140
Index   147

Contents   ix

PREFACE

This volume was written primarily for teachers—for this teacher in particular as a nostalgic souvenir during a leave of absence from the classroom. I have tried to include as many examples as possible from the children's work, so that parents and people-lovers also can enjoy this collection.

Teachers have little time, so I am going to try to save precious moments with the basic assumption: if you are looking at this book, you are "my kind of teacher." You seek new ideas to enrich the classroom experiences for yourself as well as for your students.

The process of experimentation and growth, which I call creativity, is more important than the end product. In the eyes of the beholder or audience, creativity does not necessarily imply originality. Creativity is a process within the individual, really measurable only in terms of his own development. Some teachers promote this growth by a relaxed and loving atmosphere in the classroom, which in turn leads to the discovery of unique talent or originality.

It is not easy to find the key to each child. To do so requires large amounts of insight, patience, and inventiveness. The first two qualities (which demand self analysis) are beyond my reach. However, I can offer some suggestions to promote invention—to add enjoyment and experimentation, possibly a basic philosophy, to your "language program."

Each teacher has to develop his own system.

In the beginning, invention often takes the form of adaptation, of choosing the right material for a child or a class. It is necessary to be an eclectic schoolteacher, one who dares to expand or to modify ideas, even to throw them away. (Teaching resembles writing a novel. Once an idea has been completed, it is difficult to throw it away—no matter how bad or irrelevant it is.) I keep my own notes on file cards, because they are easy to sort into categories or calendars. (My lesson-plan "book" is actually a file box.) Reappraisals are also less painful, because I simply weed out individual file cards.

M. Y. G.

Claremont, California

ACKNOWLEDGMENTS

Many people, young and older, have contributed to this book: students and their enthusiastic parents, experienced colleagues, delightful friends, loved relatives. It is impossible to acknowledge them all. Three sets of Muses in particular cannot go unnamed: Professor and Mrs. Chitoshi Yanaga, understanding parents who have always encouraged the lesser scholars in the family; Mrs. Billie Vincent, a beautiful person and a teacher I wish I had known in elementary school; and Lawrence George, a patient husband who is never too busy with The Law to help with The Book.

M. Y. G.

LANGUAGE ART: An Ideabook

INTRODUCTION

Jerome Bruner reports, "One of the conclusions of the 1959 Woods Hole Conference of the National Academy of Sciences . . . was that any subject can be taught to anybody at any age in some form that is honest."[1] I strongly agree. Adults tend to underestimate the thinking ability of children. And sadder still, teachers usually underestimate themselves.

The ideas in this book are the result of direct experience, inspired by lively groups of children in a nongraded school. I worked mainly in a self-contained classroom, sharing the room and the class with another teacher. Our students ranged in age from nine to twelve years; in the range of ability there was a much wider spread. Most of the children stayed with us for two or three years, according to plan. Therefore I was motivated to develop new material that would continually challenge them.

From this direct experience, four concepts emerged:

1. *In order to have a rich language program, subjects need to be interrelated.* Written work cannot exist in an atmosphere of skills and grammar

[1] Jerome S. Bruner, *On Knowing: Essays for the Left Hand*, p. 108. Later, Bruner repeats "there is an appropriate version of any skill or knowledge that may be imparted at whatever age one wishes to begin teaching." *(Toward a Theory of Instruction*, p. 35.)

1

only. It thrives on content and on a feeling of purpose that comes from handling provocative thoughts—"honest work" rather than busy work. Developing a sense of intellectual integrity can be fun, and rather subliminal, too.

To flourish, a language program—or for that matter a class—must be relaxed. The best writing came from casual afternoons when the children had been given a block of time to use for reading, writing, and art. The children had a clear idea of the "directions" and chose when they wanted to write. Often the writing grew out of their reading or art, as the children loosened up. (To write well, people need to unwind and jot down thoughts daily for varying periods of time.) Too frequently, the teacher can get worked up to a pitch of missionary zeal about a lesson ("Let's do this . . .") without considering the physical state of the children after lunch and lunch recess on the playground. Everyone needs time to digest, ideas as well as food. Each child should set his own pace, if honest creativity and not teacher-oriented work is the goal.

While teachers worry about perking up their curriculum, there are also times when classroom work needs to slow down. School is only part of the day for children who are loaded with activities after three o'clock. If pressures outside the classroom are great, then assignments or even "creativity" ought to relax. Reading outdoors under a tree alone or with a group is a great release valve. Even not reading serves its purpose. Unless a program is flexible to human needs, it becomes a ritual which breeds compulsiveness rather than creativity.

In general, I try to limit homework to work that has not been finished in class time or to meaningful tasks like research. If parents bear down on me for more paperwork "to prepare the children for junior high," I usually tell them that their children have been working hard in school for seven hours, which is more than enough for anyone. After-school hours should be exploratory and rambunctious. If the parents persist, I assign thirty minutes of reading daily, so that the teacher and the student can be left alone. Homework not only drains the student, but also the teacher, who, ideally, should read all the work a child does.

2. *Fun is an essential ingredient.* Fun stimulates a deeper involvement and a greater desire to communicate. For ordinary children skills such as handwriting or paragraphing improve when the need to communicate becomes strong enough.

Fun does not come in a tidy package to hand out to the students. It grows out of enthusiasm and eccentricity. The teacher needs to enjoy his

2   INTRODUCTION

native tongue, to play around with new notions, to try some of his assignments himself. Children are quite tolerant of adults. They appreciate earnest efforts to write haiku or to say original tongue twisters. They do not need to see all of the shy teacher's products. The knowledge that the teacher is also experimenting usually suffices.

Gimmicks are great, if they do not hamper the teacher. Tape recorders are very useful for the reluctant writers or the time-consuming hams. The children do just as well pretending they are tape recorders or secretaries and taking dictation from a partner. (Good exercise in aural skills for foreign-language dictations!) Typewriters encourage participation. There should be a place in every classroom for the teacher or children to bang out their ideas without disturbing anyone. Felt-tip pens are handier. Children cannot resist being inventive with all those bright, wet colors. Television is a medium outside of the classroom that children can use. With a little imagination the pattern of TV consuming the child's mind can be reversed.

3. *Reading is another prerequisite.* The teacher must read to the children, for the children and for himself. Ideas for creative writing leap out of the most amazing places. As the astute schoolmaster in *Wheel on the School* says, "Look . . . where one could be and where one couldn't possibly be."[2] Hence *The New Yorker, Mad,* and *Playboy* join the list of my resources, headed by colleagues, poets, and educators.

4. *Above all, sincere praise is necessary.* In written as well as spoken words, the teacher should encourage the writer. Specific comments, rather than mass-produced pleasantries, are vital to good writing and good friendships. In order for the children to give of themselves, they must know and trust the teacher. The teacher has to make the relationship two-sided by being warm, not smothering; supportive and accessible, not obtrusive. The adult has to emerge as a personality, someone real who feels happy and sad, angry and calm.

Publishing all of the children's work is intrinsic praise. Every possible moment of teacher-aide time was used to immortalize hastily scribbled goodies. The children loved to see their work in print, thanks to "their secretary," as well as to know that the teacher really cared.

What follows will remain in much clearer focus for the reader if these four concepts are constantly kept in mind: (1) interrelated subjects, (2) imaginative fun, (3) variety in outside reading, (4) sincere praise.

[2] Meindert de Jong, *The Wheel on the School*, p. 37.

part one

PROSE

Prose usually comes more naturally than poetry to today's children. It is a mixed blessing, at once a scourge and a gift. Children are often un-aware of style and unity in their ramblings. Their thinking, hence their writing, is fuzzy and uncontrolled. Good writing communicates in a terse, yet specific manner. In this section I suggest several lines of attack, ranging from the serious to the whimsical.

chapter one

THE CONSTRUCTED SITUATION

Giving the children a concrete experience or real artifact creates a situation in which they are confronted with the task of defining and redefining their reactions. The teacher poses an intriguing problem for the children, rather than imposing an adult definition.

FIELD TRIPS

Field trips are a good example. Excursions should always have a focus —a meaningful quest—so that they become central to the language program rather than peripheral and time-killing. Scouting an exhibit beforehand with a friend is good preparation for a teacher. The trips are also more satisfying for the children if there is a variety of approaches rather than the standard "What did you like best?" For example, strolls to local art galleries at the Claremont Colleges followed these themes: (for verbal response) "What do you think Pop Art is?" "What are your impressions of Impressionism?" (for non-verbal response) "Sketch anthropomorphic, zoomorphic, and geometric motifs from the American Indian rugs and baskets." "Sketch the shape of a 'pot' you like at the Scripps Invitational Ceramics Show." The children were earnest and enthusiastic because they knew these were "real issues," not condescending tasks. One fourth grader wrote three couplets about a trio of paintings at a special Kandinsky exhibit:

Untitled

A painting, a square
A checkerboard, a glare.

Arrangement

A ship, some lightning
A cloud, very frightening.

Arrangement No. 2

A square, a swerve
A circle, a curve.

[Philip F., age 10]

ANIMALS

Animals in the classroom are excellent subjects for writing. Fish, rats, mice, guinea pigs, rabbits, ducks, a monkey, and a year-old baby boy have all "sat" for the class who drew and observed them. Seymour, the capuchin monkey, was the most fun. The children, keeping journals, watched him closely. An article appeared in the class newspaper:

We Observe Seymour the Monkey

Differences from humans:

He has a tail and he doesn't talk. He uses his teeth for unusual things. He likes to chew on things (paintbrushes!) He uses a squeaky sound to communicate. He uses his long tail like a hand because he has a pad on the end. His feet are much smaller than humans. He doesn't have eyelashes. Walks on fours.

Similarities to humans:

He has the same kind of ears. He has fingernails and toenails. He throws

8   Part One: PROSE

fits. He stands on his hind feet. He likes to play. He amuses himself. He sucks his thumb.

The younger children also commented with insight and humor: for example, "Seymour is a monkey. An undersized Tarzan. Seymour likes to hide." [Ted E., age 7]

Once they knew him well, the children tried to imagine how Seymour looked at life in the classroom. Their descriptions were rich and varied —alas, unpreserved. The shift to Seymour's outlook was a good exercise in viewpoint, an important technique discussed in the next section.

ARTIFACTS

An artifact like an ordinary penny can also provide a new experience in the classroom. Related to the social studies, here are some of the discoveries made by amateur archeologists "from the year 4000 A.D.":

Found a Penny ...

"In God We Trust"—probably a very religious culture.
Is the figure with the beard their god?
Is the number the man's age? Or when it was made?
There is a building on it. Was it a temple?
"E Pluribus Unum" is the name of the man. Very curly hair, big chin.
Two odd plants, now extinct.
One cent? Maybe a game piece or a counting object. Used as a sign of trust? Could be a button. A medal? Money?
This object is 5/8 in. wide. Round. There are forty-one letters on it. Copper. Tastes bad.

Postscript: The archeologists kept the artifact, even though one girl protested—"but teachers are poor!"

A telephone directory is another everyday object which excites interest in social studies.[1] If each child has his own book, he can pore leisurely through the yellow pages ("Let your fingers do the walking") and construct an interesting picture of the contemporary habits of the native. The street listings often indicate the type of community. For instance, Claremont is a small college town with main north-south streets or avenues, or places named College, Mills, Yale, Harvard, Cambridge, Berkeley, Oxford,

[1] For further ideas, see Clements, Tabachnick, and Fielder, *Social Study*.

Dartmouth. Only a few of the streets give some indication of the more rugged location of the town: Mountain Avenue, Foothill Boulevard, Indian Hill Boulevard, Arrow Highway.

Peter Blake in *God's Own Junkyard* creates striking visual juxtapositions of beauty and horror, which fascinate the children and stimulate them to look around for man-made successes and atrocities. In their evaluations, they are stricter than the local architectural review board!

Having children for at least two years in the classroom is exciting, because the teacher can see some of these ideas ferment. The children note changes in Claremont since their arrival and search for architectural forms like the arch, the dome, the post and lintel. They become very involved in the community, constantly bringing in examples to support their opinions.

Two packages of animal crackers were worth their weight in gold—the best 20-cent investment I have made in creative writing, even cheaper than the penny episode. Like the cent, the cracker had its own intrinsic reward. The author gobbled up his artifact as soon as I had seen the story and often an accompanying picture. The boys kept coming back for another "assignment," a different animal. One hungry young writer produced these amusing remarks:

1. Kangaroos jump so high that sometimes when they come down, the baby jumps out.

2. This is a funny, very funny animal. It is a lamb. When I want some wool, I peel it off with my teeth!

3. Elephants are giants to atoms, although atoms are not scared of them. Atoms help feed elephants.

[Seth M., age 6]

Rather than being isolated exercises, these experiences pave the way for further forays into the realm of viewpoint (the next segment) and into the domain of poetry. Since the latter is in the second part of this book, I will now make the connection between poetry and the penny, the telephone book, or the animal cracker. Children learn to use ordinary objects to make extraordinary observations. This concept, compressed further, turns into one plausible definition of poetry—"the ordinary becomes extraordinary."

chapter two

VIEWPOINT

A teacher aims towards broadening the experiences and viewpoints of his students, while focusing the children's awareness of specifics. At best, it is a delicate balance. Unless the children begin to understand different points of view in a literary sense, they can never fathom cultural biases in social studies or prejudice in politics. They need to learn to shift attitudes while they are still able. Otherwise, a large part of the thinking process—of intellectual growth—will be closed to them.

ROLE PLAYING

Viewpoint can be studied best by doing. Children instinctively recognize viewpoint: playing, they invent and assume roles. Often this activity is continued in school with dramatics. In the hands of many teachers, however, performances tend to be pushed to perfection for the audience—overproduced. The investment of time hardly seems justified as a language experience. Impromptu plays and pantomime like acting out sayings from

Ben Franklin's Wit and Wisdom[1] are more rewarding, particularly for extroverts.

Very little is usually done with viewpoint in private, written work, yet the children enjoy such experiments. They take the viewpoint of an insect or animal and produce descriptions like this:

I am a chipmunk and I'd like to talk about the fabulous thing called the golf course. You can do anything in it. You can play catch with a walnut or take a walk, throw things on the heads of those big animals called humans, play hide'n'seek and hide in the holes. It's real fun to climb up the flagpoles. It's also fun to hide those white awful tasting nuts in sandy places or in those lakes . . .

[Beth B., age 10]

I the Giant Brontosaurus walk around. I look at the water this way: a rescue from the terrible Tyrannosaurus Rex. The water gives me protection from this wild beast that is water shy. I can wade deep and the water keeps my thirty tons of meat up. I can stretch my neck out of the water to breathe.

I also look at the water as a place to get the plants on which I live—lilies, moss and ferns. I eat all day to live.

[Holly B., age 11]

A Horse's Point of View of a Saddle

Ick, it is like an undershirt, a sweatshirt, a jacket, long underwear and long pants on a H O T day. A belt wrapped so tight you can hardly breathe.

[Diane S., age 11]

Other children have written brief stories about *The Travels of . . . (a Penny*, or *a Shoesole*, or *a Stamp*). Here are some samples of their openings:

I am a stamp. It is very tiring. You can't go where you wish . . .

It was a hot day in the San Francisco mint where I was born. The year was 1909 and little did I know that in a few decades I would be very rare and known as the 1909 VDB "S" . . .

[1] Joseph Crawhall, illustrator.

Mrs. Smith put me on a letter. Thud. She just dropped me in that stinky mailbox. After a while I make a few friends. I meet George Washington and Abraham Lincoln, too . . .

BIOGRAPHY

A second aspect of viewpoint can be demonstrated by studying biography or comparing the biographies[2] of a well-known figure like Benjamin Franklin. In alternate years the children concentrated on four of the Founding Fathers, using a challenging unit developed by Mrs. Billie Vincent at Sycamore School. Her ideas provided the background for another concept which I pursued. The procedure was simple. The teacher read an interesting Franklin biography by Clara Judson[3] to the class. On their own, the students read another biography on Franklin by Meadowcroft,[4] its chief virtue being availability in paperback. During their reading, they had a sheet of specific questions that I had prepared and furnished them in ditto form.

BIOGRAPHY

Comparison of books by Judson and Meadowcroft

1. Do the facts agree in both books? If you spot any ''mistakes,'' check the information in a third book on Franklin or an encyclopedia.

2. Compare two tellings of the same event. Are they exactly the same? If not, what things are different? Can you see any reason for the difference?

3. Should the writer tell the whole truth about a man? Is it honest to leave out some of the facts? (In other words, should a biography be completely true or beautiful?)

4. Which book did you like better? Why? (Please think about writing style.)

DUE: October 3rd for discussion

---

[2] James Clifford, ed., *Biography as an Art.*

[3] Clara Ingalls Judson, *Benjamin Franklin.*

[4] Enid L. Meadowcroft, *The Story of Benjamin Franklin.*

After the reading the children compared the two books in a discussion guided by my questions. As they talked, I wrote their contributions on the blackboard for them to observe, editing and organizing on the spot. Both my questions and my notes of the class discussion are reproduced. My format for the guiding questions was a set of notes on file cards, developed from earlier class readings of Judson. The discussion notes were kept on file cards also, later reorganized as presented here.

NOTES ON DISCUSSION ABOUT FRANKLIN

Comparison of Biographies

Characteristics	Reason
Meadowcroft	
More story	TO
Description overdone (i.e. book starts with	APPEAL
''It was a bright and sunny day.'' Was it	TO
really?)	CHILDREN
More of childhood, grandchildren	
Fewer faults revealed	BEN
Smallpox blamed for son's death, not lack	IS
of vaccination (as in Judson where Franklin	MORE HERO
did not believe in innoculation)	THAN HUMAN.
	MODEL
Fewer events, dates	FOR
Skipped death--''he went to sleep''	CHILDREN
Fewer ideas	
Junto, a thinking group, underplayed	
The writer interferes more in this biography.	
She tries to shape it to teach children.	
Judson	
More fact, history, humor (Silence Dogood)	
More of manhood	
Real person, well-rounded. ''Tearing off	
wing'' as well as good qualities mentioned	
Better conversations	

The majority of the class preferred Judson and biographies that tell all. A stalwart few admitted that when they are famous they would prefer to have some of the facts of their lives left out!

Whenever the class discussed an "issue" or an assignment, I took notes on the blackboard. Several scribes copied them down on paper, so I could take the notes home and make dittoes. I gave each child a copy of the notes on the following day for his folder. It let the class see and own the results of the discussions. It was also good public relations for the parents, so they could know some of the goings on.

PROPAGANDA

As another exercise in viewpoint, the class ventured into the realm of propaganda. They followed the newspaper intently and posted clippings, particularly about Viet Nam. They published a shocking edition of the classroom newspaper for Back to School Night. Until the browser read the fine print at the end of each article, he wondered about the local news. The captions fell into one of these seven categories[5]:

1. *Name Calling*. The propagandist tries to get us to hate or fear someone or something, by giving "bad names" to these people, groups, nations, and beliefs which he wants us to dislike.

2. *Glittering Generalities*. The propagandist tries to get us to like someone or a program by using words that appeal to us, such as *truth, freedom, liberty,* and *progress*. (His idea is to get the reader to accept the generalities without checking the facts.)

3. *Transfer*. The propagandist takes something we respect and connects it with his program, so we will like his program. "Our country's heroes" might be that something. He tries to make us believe that these heroes would or would not like his program.

4. *Testimonial*. The propagandist may hire famous people to "like" something. Therefore we should like it?

5. *Plain folks*. Public figures may try to get us to like them (not because of their program) but because they are just "plain folks among the neighbors."

---

[5] Simplified version of definitions from the Institute of Propaganda Analysis, done by Mrs. Billie Vincent. There is also a game called "The Propaganda Game" (Wiff 'N Proof, Box 71, New Haven, Connecticut), which deals with these categories.

6. Card Stacking. The propagandist exaggerates, tells half truths, leaves out the facts. He doesn't tell the other side.

7. Bandwagon. "Everybody's doing it, so we should, too." It must be the right thing to do?

In addition, the class compared reporting of the same event, culled from a selection of local newspapers. The children also drew their own political cartoons, using a subconscious backlog of national and international events. Elections provided a wealth of material. (As long as the teacher remains a "political eunuch" in front of the group, the children can passionately participate in the elections. They do so anyway behind the scenes, no matter how much the teacher tries to restrain partisan politics. Only the World Series competes in intensity.)

HOAXES

Hoaxes, Heroes, and Hogwash[6] is in a slightly more neutral territory related to propaganda. For part one of this adventure, *Hoaxes* by Curtis MacDougall is good background. The pictures are fascinating. For discussion, I prepared a ditto for the children based on my reading.

My ditto sheet has some references that were made clear to the students at the time they used it, but may need to be clarified here. The event given as an example in 2.b was the distribution by a major news service of a picture supposedly taken of Adolf Hitler as a baby; it was in fact a retouched photograph of a two-year-old Connecticut boy. The background of 3.a is the fact that genuine photos of Lincoln as an orator and as a family man, before he became President, are relatively rare. On the other hand, alleged photos of the sort are relatively common—men in darkrooms have borrowed heads and bodies to display the standard and expected postures of family devotion and public eloquence. The Mecklenburg Declaration of Independence mentioned in 3.b may have been genuine or may have been a hoax; but the first printed draft dates from 1800 and at the time of publication was acknowledged to be from memory.

The event cited in 3.c is a classic in recent history. On October 30, 1938, a radio drama program directed by Orson Welles presented a show based on H. G. Wells's old science-fiction novel *The War of the Worlds*. All over the United States, millions of people took the broadcast for factual

---

[6] Mary George, *Hoaxes, Heroes, and Hogwash* (unpublished; 1964).

1. What is a hoax?

2. Why do people create hoaxes?

    a. Personal reasons: fame and fortune (e.g. P. T. Barnum)

    b. Impersonal reasons: to advance the ''Cause''

        e.g. National heroes like George Washington, shaped by Parson Weems

        e.g. International villains like Hitler (alleged picture of nasty baby Adolf)

3. Why do people believe?

    a. Ignorance or indifference

        e.g. Lack of photographs of Lincoln with family or as an orator provided incentive to retouch pictures. Few people knew the difference.

    b. Pride

        e.g. National pride in forefathers
        Local pride (Mecklenburg Declaration of Independence, still celebrated on anniversary of May 20, 1775, spotlights North Carolina rather than Pennsylvania.)

    c. Climate of the times

        e.g. Warlike mood (1938)--Orson Welles' version of War of the Worlds by H. G. Welles seemed real to radio audience, causing a widespread panic.

news and panicked. Here in all likelihood no hoax was intended—but what happened was very much like one.

It would be an interesting shift from the lecture-discussion technique, if a teacher used the record of this broadcast[7] and played it without comment to begin a unit on Hoaxes. The situation in the classroom would hardly duplicate a casual scene beside the radio on a Sunday evening in a

---

[7] It is alleged that the broadcasting company destroyed all transcriptions at the time to suppress evidence that might have supported lawsuits. A copy survived nonetheless. Recently it was issued by Audio Rarities (LPA 2355). Excerpts from Welles's script are published in *The Golden Web* by Erik Barnouw. The entire script can be found in *Invasion from Mars* by Hadley Cantril.

prewar living room. However, it still might be conducive to a comparison of life, then and now. The stylistic differences of news reporting are striking. (Just imagine H. V. Kaltenborn and Walter Winchell, as opposed to Chet Huntley and David Brinkley!)

"The panic had one immediate effect on broadcast policy. Interruptions for fictional news bulletins became taboo in broadcast drama."[8] Using another well-known example—the shout of a false alarm "Fire" in a crowded theater—can inspire fervid discussion of the First Amendment! What are the limits of freedom? It is amazing how involved children can become in such essentials.

HEROES

Although it seems a bit harsh, the propaganda approach can augment a study of heroes, among whom are our founding fathers.

Some school districts may not tolerate such "deviations" from flag waving. (It is always wise to check beforehand with the principal and gain his real approval in advance of any possible controversy. He then can be an informed and understanding advocate, rather than a bewildered administrator who gives nominal support.) In a democratic country, it is a shame for such conditions of insecurity to exist.

To protect the nation's image, elementary schoolteachers often suppress reality or dissent. I feel that is the more dangerous course, especially in this epoch. Children raised on a diet of fairy-tale history will later reject the American past as delusions. They will be enriched by beginning at an earlier age to evaluate heroes and their legends. Their heritage will be more tangible, more real. They will also be able to laugh at the "jokes" of the past. (Too often, teachers are deadly earnest. The responsibility for thirty-five children can make anyone deadly!)

The cartoonists of the past can relieve the teacher of the burden of responsibility. The few extant political cartoons of George Washington and Abraham Lincoln are excellent vehicles for the study of viewpoint. Again I exhibit a copy of my notes for the discussion. They were illustrated with pictures that do not appear here, from William Murrell's *A History of American Humor* (New York, Whitney Museum, 1933).

---

[8] "How Orson Welles' 'War of the Worlds' Shocked Nation Into a State of Panic," *Los Angeles Times*, July 13, 1969, p. 18 of Calendar section.

HEROES

Political cartoons of George Washington are extremely rare, not because he was spared from ridicule by contemporaries but because he was spared by zealous censors in recent times.

Viewpoint

1. How do you feel about George Washington--if you are a soldier under his command? Does Gilbert Stuart's portrait represent your feelings towards him?

2. How do you feel about George Washington--if you are a political rival? Would you take advantage of the rumor supposedly uttered by Mrs. Washington on her deathbed that the old General was actually a woman? Somebody leaped at the chance in a cartoon called ''Mrs. General Washington Bestowing Thirteen Stripes on Britannia.''

3. How do you feel about George Washington--if you are a British subject? An Englishman caricatured Washington as an armadillo, Hancock an ass, Adams a fox and Putnam a boar.

George Washington had his ups and downs as a hero and as a human.

1. During what periods in history do you think flattering cartoons were drawn?

1824--General Lafayette's visit to America?

1848--War with Mexico?

1932--200th anniversary of birth, publicized by Sol Bloom? (Flattering cartoons apparently occur during wartime or bankrupt periods when there is a need to be reminded of the country's rugged past.)

2. When do you think the low periods occurred?

During the Jeffersonian period when his party was trying to ruin Federalists?

During the Civil War and after Lincoln was martyred?

During the 1920's when ''smartness and cynicism reigned''?

2. Viewpoint   19

TELEVISION

Experience with hogwash is the most fun, because it fits a childish preoccupation—television. Also, in this age of McLuhan (or post-McLuhan?) it is intriguing for the teacher to observe the viewing habits of his class. Each child keeps a journal of television programs he ordinarily watches during one week, carefully noting the number and type of commercials for each show. (It is a good idea to do this early in the year before the reruns bore even the youngest audience.) Daily the class pools its information and keeps a joint record. The very few who do not own a set or who may be banned from seeing television for a week can help the teacher with keeping the record and making the ditto sheets. At the end of the week, the children receive a copy of the class journal and a set of questions (see the example).

TELEVISION ASSIGNMENT: LOOK FOR PATTERNS

1. Pick a sponsor and see what programs it likes to finance.

2. What products are ''sold'' at certain times of the day, e.g. dinnertime, bedtime.

3. Try to decide by the advertising only which programs are designed for:
(a) kids, (b) teenagers, (c) adult women, (d) adult men, (e) elderly people.

4. Ask your own questions, too, and find the answers.

Written conclusions due for discussion on Monday.

The results can be impressive. For example, the children discovered from our limited sampling that:

Question 1

    a. Dogfood and cigarettes tend to sponsor comedies.

    b. Beer and cars sponsored adventure, sports. (Hard liquor not advertised on television; ads mainly in magazines.)

    c. Detergents on exciting shows, adventures.

    d. Mouthwash and stomach remedies sponsored a variety of shows. Timing—after dinner—was uppermost.

e. Maxwell House also sponsored a variety of shows in the same time slot—8:00-8:30 p.m. daily. Just in time for the after-dinner cup of coffee?

Question 2

a. Soap before dinner.

b. Toothpaste after meals.

c. Cereals on kiddie shows.

d. Cigarettes from 7:30-9:00 p.m. daily, mainly on adventures "where the tension builds up."

e. Wax on Friday before weekend cleaning.

Question 3

One boy noticed that "our TV log is based on our class's viewing habits; therefore it is weighted toward kids." The class still had fun with the question, but the results are too lengthy to include here. In general, the children concluded that television commercials greatly underestimate their audience.

The possibilities have only been lightly tapped. Children find projects involving market research most natural and engrossing. In fact, they are experts who tag along to the supermarket, and absorb endless amounts of advertising from various media. For more on the "moppet market," the *Reader's Guide to Periodical Literature* is a gold mine. The *Saturday Review of Literature* gives out annual advertising awards in April, a perfect finale for a study of advertising (almost like predicting the Academy or Newbery Awards)!

chapter three

OPEN-ENDED
QUESTIONS

So far my suggestions have dealt with the available world, largely in the area of social studies. The projects have been long-term and loaded with import. A language program needs to be securely based, but it also needs to be playful and spontaneous. I have a number of "one-night stands" that were originally devised for substitute teachers. I "spent" the plans, rather than hoarding them for strangers, because I wanted the children to identify the assignments with me. Hence, I kept creating and collecting new ideas that eventually evolved into a category called "Questions." Sometimes the questions were coordinated with the calendar or class reading, as was Question 1. The situation became highly meaningful and intimate.

Question 1. On January 31 we had just finished reading *Wrinkle in Time.* It also happened to be the anniversary of the first launching of an

American satellite in 1958. The children were asked "What is time?" "What is space?"

> Time is the tick-tock of a clock,
> The years and years that make a rock.
> It's the hours you wait to go somewhere,
> The month it takes to grow your hair.
> Time is the seconds before you win the race,
> The minutes it takes to wash your face.
> Time is about us everywhere
> And if it stops, I hope I'm not there.

[Sue Belle S., age 11]

Space . . . a little room, the air we breathe, the little space in which I mark my answers, the stars and the planets, the place between me and my shirt.

[Howie U., age 11]

SENSORY QUESTIONS

Questions 2 and 3. These next two questions are related:

> What is the quietest sound you know?
> What is the noisiest sound you know?

They could be asked as a pair or independently, depending on the mood of the moment. I asked the younger children to answer the first question, when the small group was huddled around me and very still. I took dictation from the six-year-olds. I posed both questions in the midst of turmoil, a usual condition in our classroom of older children. The children found quiet corners or shady trees to meditate.

What is the quietest sound you know?

Teacher's voice	People walking barefeet
Snowflakes	Tooth falling out
Birds flapping their wings	Plants growing
A glider	Cats walking
Grasshoppers	An eardrum
Hatching eggs	Someone picking a flower
Nobody at home	Eyes blinking

[Various kindergarteners]

3. Open-Ended Questions 23

Dog whistle
A whisper
A bee, a flea
Mice
Teachers?

[Ted E., age 9]

A rat sleeping in a nest of kleenex.

[Laurie Z., age 11]

A bowling alley. It should really be the quietest sound because you can hear a pin drop.

[Denis F., age 11]

What is the noisiest sound you know?

On top of Mt. Whitney—the unexpected barking of a chihuahua.

[Cindy K., age 11]

The noisiest thing I know is when I'm quiet and everyone else is yelling and screaming.

[Dena B., age 11]

The clarinet when you play wrong keys or notes.

[Laurie Z., age 11]

Do You Hear What I Hear?[1] is an excellent companion for this assignment. It gives examples of harsh and sweet sounds, long and short sounds, loud and quiet sounds. One of my colleagues shared this book with her kindergarteners, who painted and dictated their own stories about sounds happy and sad, friendly and lonely, excited and mad.

The Quiet-Noisy Book[2] is another good book. Questions like "Was it butter melting?" will motivate the youngest writers.

Questions 4 and 5. One summer I took two things to class, an abalone shell and a conch shell. In them, the primary children saw and heard many marvels. I preserved a few samples of each.

[1] Helen Borten, *Do You Hear What I Hear?*
[2] Margaret Wise Brown, *The Quiet-Noisy Book.*

Part One: PROSE

What do you see in the abalone shell?

Oilspots   Steps of Time
Rainbow   Craters on the moon
    Twin Peaks of Mt. Whitney

What do you hear in the conch shell?

People whispering
Lullaby
Crabs walking on sand
Song from the *Bridge on the River Kwai*

Nina Walter in *Let Them Write Poetry* suggests a lovely procedure for little ones composing poems, based on the sounds in a conch shell.

IDENTITY QUESTIONS: OBJECTS

Questions 6. An old stand-by continues the mariner theme: "If you were stranded on a deserted island, what one book would you want?"

If I were stranded on a desert island, I would like to read a book like *The Little Prince*, because it is about a man who gets stranded on a desert and almost dies of thirst. He gets some water later, so it would keep up my hopes better.

[Adam K., age 11]

When I was stranded on a deserted island with only a knife and my clothes, I wished I had a *Boy Scout Handbook* instead of the Dick Tracy comic which I had.

[Randy F., age 10]

Variations would be: "What would you say in a note that was going to be put in a bottle and cast into the sea?" "If you had to choose ten things to put into a time capsule, what would they be?"

Question 7. It was May 1, Lei Day in Hawaii, when I sprang this question. The idea is good in the forty-nine states, where it is difficult to find the correct spelling, let alone the meaning: "What is a humuhumu-nuku-nuku-a-pua'a?"

A chant that the Hawaiians used to sing.

3. Open-Ended Questions   25

A cheese sandwich with onions, raw eggs, fish sticks and steak sauce.

A purple polka-dotted lizard that lives on the Hawaiian Islands and swims in volcanoes.

Supercalifragilisticexpialidotious.

A person who says things twice when he says humunukuapa.

It is anticlimatic to admit that humuhumu-nukunuku-a-pua'a is a small tropical fish, a variety of the humuhumu, swimming in the Pacific waters.

IDENTITY QUESTIONS: SELF

Question 8. "Who am I?" is a very good assignment for the beginning of the year. The question establishes individual identity, at the same time it cements group feelings of solidarity. (It would be fun to try it at the end of the year to see how well the children really know each other.) The class members enjoyed selecting difficult clues about themselves. The varying levels of sophistication were most revealing.

We live in an old house built in 1903. Every main house that my father and mother have lived in has been torn down and the one we are in now almost was.

[Charles R., age 10]

I was born in Taipei, Taiwan. I went to school in Hong Kong. Right now we live in an apartment in Claremont. The landlord is a big fat miser. He is trying to get rid of our dog, whose name is Sambo but he isn't black. Once my friend and I were playing with the hose outside and he came along and told us to turn off the water. (He pays for the water but he raised the rent already.) We're thinking of moving.

[Denis F., age 11]

I was born in Pomona Valley Hospital. I have flown over 4,000 miles and gone 200 by train. My ancestor signed the Declaration of Independence. My great great grandfather invented one of the first blimps and my great grandfather invented a cash machine.

[Scott F., age 10]

I was born in Boston, Mass. Then I moved to Calif. when I was half the age I am now. We have a 1965 car. We have had four cars in my lifetime. My favorite singing group is the Beatles.

[Beth B., age 10]

The next three questions capitalize on the human fascination for significant birth signs. Playing around with astrology, as well as astronomy, the students gave their answers to these queries.

Question 9. (a) Were you born under the right sign? Why? (b) What is your horoscope for "tomorrow"?

Information on the zodiac, based on a book by Louis MacNeice[3] was charted. The children pored over the personality traits of each sign and noted celebrities connected with them before they wrote the following:

Scorpio

I should have been born under this month. I am aggressive and stubborn and a lot like Mussolini.

[Francis D., age 10]

Taurus

I think I was born in a good sign because he's a tower of strength and furious. I don't care too much about slow and long suffering.

Horoscope: To be real strong and be able to throw and play sports real good.

[Jim D., age 11]

Virgo

I think I should be born under Sagittarius the Archer because I love the wide open spaces.

Virgo, I hope, will get a year vacation. The hunting season will be open wherever he goes.

[Steve S., age 10]

Libra

Horoscope: Go to a Chinese restaurant. Your fortune cookie will tell you the rest.

Sagittarius

I think I am fit for that because I tell the truth and love to explore. Sometimes I act half-human.

[Cathy E., age 11]

[3] Louis MacNeice, *Astrology.*

3. Open-Ended Questions

Make good actors, shy, gentle, drink, lie, loveable. It doesn't fit me at all, except that I lie and make a good actor.

Horoscope: You will win $1,000,000 on the TV show "Let's Go to the Races." Your bike will rust.

[Denis F., age 11]

Question 10. The Chinese and Japanese have a twelve-year cycle of symbols. Each year has an animal with certain characteristics that are quite different from Western interpretation. The children closely examined the following chart before they answered the questions: "Were you born in the right year? Why?" "Does the information match the other members of your family?"

1900, 1912, 1924, 1936, 1948, and 1960 are years of the Rat: cute and harmless.

1901, 1913, 1925, 1937, 1949, and 1961 are years of the Cow or Bull: good worker. Nice but not smart.

1902, 1914, 1926, 1938, 1950, and 1962 are years of the Tiger: strong.

1903, 1915, 1927, 1939, 1951, and 1963 are years of the Rabbit: quick and energetic.

1904, 1916, 1928, 1940, 1952, and 1964 are years of the Dragon: happy.

1905, 1917, 1929, 1941, 1953, and 1965 are years of the Snake: lucky.

1906, 1918, 1930, 1942, 1954, and 1966 are years of the Horse: fast but not smart. Girls are not good marriage prospects.

1907, 1919, 1931, 1943, 1955, and 1967 are years of the Sheep: quiet.

1908, 1920, 1932, 1944, 1956, and 1968 are years of the Monkey: smart.

1909, 1921, 1933, 1945, 1957, and 1969 are years of the Chicken: lucky.

1910, 1922, 1934, 1946, 1958, and 1970 are years of the Dog: spy or informer.

1911, 1923, 1935, 1947, 1959, and 1971 are years of the Boar: better than strong tiger.

The answers were fascinating. The children started by looking at themselves and their immediate families, then extended their observation to include friends and heroes. For a semester, they continued to share their insights.

Part One: PROSE

Question 11. Based on an old rhyme, this question may require a little research, referring to old calendars to find the weekday of birth: "Were you born on the right day? Why?"

> Monday's child is fair of face,
> Tuesday's child is full of grace,
> Wednesday's child is full of woe,
> Thursday's child has far to go,
> Friday's child is loving and giving,
> Saturday's child works hard for a living,
> And a child that's born on the Sabbath day
> Is fair and wise and good and gay.

My pupils have not yet pursued this question, so I cannot display their answers.

SUNDRY QUESTIONS

Question 12. What Do You Say, Dear? is a delightful book,[4] concocted by Sesyle Joslin and illustrated by Maurice Sendak. It can be read to the class as motivating material. My children came up with preposterous etiquette of their own:

You are in a theater when a rhino sits on you. What do you say, dear?

—I beg your pardon.

[Andy K., age 11]

Your mother asks you to wash the dishes and your best TV show is on. What do you say, dear?

—No, thank you.

[Elvira M., age 10]

The mention of Maurice Sendak reminds me of another category which could be phrased into questions—redefinitions of everyday objects or actions. *A Hole is to Dig* by Ruth Krauss[5] and illustrated by Maurice Sendak is a collection of children's opinions as naive as my own daughter's definition of snow: "the white stuff you put your skis on." (Quite obviously she is a three-year-old from southern California!)

Along these same lines, equally amusing, are Charles Schulz's cartoon

---

[4] Sesyle Joslin, *What Do You Say, Dear?*
[5] Ruth Krauss, *A Hole Is to Dig.*

books. What teacher has not used and enjoyed *Happiness Is . . .* ? (There are counterparts that have titles beginning *Happiness Is . . .* and *Misery Is . . .*—some by other authors like Langston Hughes and Johnny Carson, and some quite definitely not for children.)

Other teachers have played around with several other queries, which I present here:

Question 13. What are your thoughts on the last day of school (before Christmas vacation)?

Question 14. If you could give a Valentine to a special person who is not living today, whom would you choose?

Question 15. Who is Loof Lirpa? (April Fool)

Question 16. If you were alone at home, what would you do? (After all kinds of bravado and fantasy, on the part of the boys in particular, one girl responded: "If I were home alone, I would sit and read because Mom would find out if I did anything.")

Question 17. The American Legion chose a rewarding topic for its annual essay contest: Five Wishes for My Country. The class predominantly wished for an end to poverty and birth defects. Here are some sets of wishes the children expressed:

1. To have all men treated equally no matter what race he or she is.
2. To give jobs to people who are unable to get them for themselves.
3. To make coins. Everyone is short of coins. The stores won't change anything.
4. To help the U.S. soldier in Viet Nam.
5. To have more homes for the homeless and orphans.

[Terry S., age 11]

1. I wish that we won't have any more war.
2. I wish there would be short hours of school.
3. I wish Mr. Kennedy were alive again.
4. I wish that one room will be for girls and the other room will be for boys.
5. ???

[Eddie G., age 11]

1. My first wish would be for people not to see beer and wine because sometimes men get killed in cars.
2. I wish we wouldn't have to pay tax in stores every time we bought something.

Part One: PROSE

3. I wish the clothes wouldn't cost so much. Like dresses, because now they cost almost two dollars.

4. I wish that colored people would have as much as other people.

5. My fifth wish is that the governor of Mexico would fix the roads.

[Alma R., age 10]

chapter four

☙

SERENDIPITY

Serendipity deserves a very special place in my book. The moments I discovered it and used it in the classroom were some of the happiest for me, as well as for the children. We had learned to relax and explore together on a playful level, verbal or visual.

Many children are afraid of written language or they become tense about adult expectations in this area. They become prissy with pencil and paper by the time they are in the upper grades. Serendipity dramatically dispels some of these fears by teasing their imagination. The children play with alphabet letters or with words on a visual level, feel comfortable, and move on to sentences. They develop a love for language which paves the way for poetry.

ALPHABET GAMES

Here are some "games" I have devised. They are to be used only as a starting point, because the real joy of serendipity is to invent an individual style based on different interests.

Game 1. Steinberg cartoons are excellent for use in the classroom. His drawings open a whole new approach to the alphabet. Even children who have been afraid of written work become intrigued and experiment with letters. The December 4, 1965, issue of *The New Yorker* magazine has a passel of goodies—marching bands, theatrical performances, domestic scenes (father *A* greeted by mother *B* and kiddies, *a* and *b*), social comments (stolid *A*, watching fancy script 𝔄 blast off, thinks LSD). The results are amazing: shortly the class becomes Super-Steinberg with a scope and humor that would surely please the artist.

Game 2. After the children are "warmed up," they can write imaginative alphabet stories using onomatopoeia, like *Mary Poppins from A to Z,*[1] or *Anna Amelia's Apteryx,*[2] or *I Love My Anteater.*[3] Bestiaries like the one by T. H. White are another recipe of these alphabet soups. The boys in particular enjoy inventing "beasties of all manner."

TONGUE-TWISTERS

Game 3. It is just a short hop to tongue twisters, to me a worthy enterprise since I read the introduction to *The Big Book of Tongue Twisters and Double Talk* by Arnold Arnold[4] "In our day, much of the word-of-mouth hand-me-downs from child to child have been interrupted by TV, comics and other passive sport. Too many children and adults now imagine play as being possible only with things. I dedicate this book to the revival of play with sounds, words and ideas. This sort of verse and play with words is the stuff of which Mother Goose is made . . . I hope that all of these will be carried forward in the hearts of the children of today, to be repeated by them, when they walk and burp the babies of tomorrow."

As a group, the children practiced these well-known tongue twisters, many of which Arnold prints:

---

[1] Pamela L. Travers, *Mary Poppins from A to Z.*
[2] Mary O'Neill, *Anna Amelia's Apteryx.*
[3] Dahlov Ipcar, *I Love My Anteater.*
[4] Arnold Arnold, *The Big Book of Tongue Twisters and Double Talk.*

4. Serendipity   33

I.

Betty Botter bought some butter.
"But," she said, "the butter's bitter;
if I put it in my batter,
it will make my batter bitter,
but a bit of better butter,
that would make my batter better."

II.

A fly and a flea flew into a flue.
Said the flea, "Fly what shall we do?"
Said the fly, "Let us flee!"
Said the flea, "Let us fly!"
So they flew through a flaw in the flue.

III.

How much wood would a woodchuck chuck
if a woodchuck could chuck wood?
He would chuck, he would, as much as he could,
and chuck as much wood as a woodchuck would
if a woodchuck could chuck wood.

IV.

He who knows not and knows not that he knows not,
 he is a fool; shun him.
He who knows not and knows that he knows not,
 he is simple; teach him.
He who knows and knows not that he knows,
 he is asleep; wake him.
He who knows and knows that he knows,
 he is wise; follow him.

V.

Theophilus Thistledown, the successful thistle sifter,
in sifting a sieve of unsifted thistles
thrust three thousand thistles through the thick of his thumb.
If, then, Theophilus Thistledown, the successful thistle sifter,
in sifting a sieve of unsifted thistles
thrust three thousand thistles through the thick of his thumb,
see that thou, in sifting a sieve of unsifted thistles,
gettest not the unsifted thistles stuck in thy tongue.

VI.

Moses supposes his toeses are roses,
But Moses supposes erroneously;
For nobody's toeses are posies of roses
As Moses supposes his toeses to be.

Then they went off and tried to write their own, with creativity conceivably contaminated by subliminal recall. I taped the results, as each child became ready. (I exercised mild censorship, something I rarely do, because the boys were testing "sh" and "f" sounds!) The tape recording was as much fun as the writing. Alas, I have only one example left, thanks to the features page of the classroom newspaper:

Does a doctor doctor a doctor according to the doctored doctor's doctrine of doctoring, or does the doctor doing the doctoring doctor the other doctor according to his own doctoring doctrine?

[Denis F., age 11]

Tongue twisters can boost other skills than enunciation. I used "Esaw Wood"[5] to demonstrate capitalization. (It was a toss-up because punctuation could be highlighted equally well.) The children were delighted by such a dramatic "grammar lesson," and almost to a man(!) they took home the ditto sheets to test the skills of their parents.

HIDDEN WORDS

Game 4. "Leadership" was another assignment which had wide circulation around the school and homes. The children were asked to make as many words as possible out of the letters in the word LEADERSHIP. I was surprised by the participation of children who hated spelling and writing. They did as well as the others, if not better. Of the three hundred and twelve words they discovered, some of the "sophisticated" ones that came up during our fiery forty-five minute discussion included *Israel, Paris, diaper, easel, Eire, lard, perish, parish, spa, Hesperia, Aries, radish, relish, Pisa, spiel, per se, Persia, seder, April, Alps, hearse, pedals, sidereal, Pharisee, reside, phrase, rile, pearls, sepal, serial, shale, ladies, sidle, leer, leper, lira, elapse, rasp, herald, shard, pi, parse, spider, desire.*

[5] See pages 54-55.

4. Serendipity   35

The March 5, 1966, issue of *The New Yorker* has a marvelous post-script—or motivation, if you like. The cartoon depicts an executive staring at a sign "THINK" across from his desk. He has made a dozen words so far—*thin, in, kit, hit, hint, tin, knit, nit, ink, it, kin, kith.* Everybody's doing it!

Game 5. Hidden words are contagious. The class[6] made up sentences that contain hidden words in categories like animals, fish, birds, insects, brand names, people. I have included all of them here, because they are fun to find, as well as to invent, in the awkward moments that sneak up in a day, whether at school or a party. These sentences were appended to the school newspaper. Like many other assignments, the children's work received larger circulation beyond the classroom. Such additions added variety and interest to the monthly tabloid.

Animals and Birds

1. Mr. Howard Vark ran for office. (Ardvark; well, aardvark)
2. All the helium balloons soared up to the sky. (Loons)
3. The sailor said, "Let down the anchor. See what you can see." (Horse)
4. The calf inched his way out of the mud. (Finch)
5. The scab at the end of my nose hurts. (Bat)
6. One is a counting number. (Gnu)
7. I went on a catamaran. (Cat)
8. Did you hear the rumor at school? (Rat)
9. School starts two weeks hence. (Hen)
10. There is no rib exercise. (Ibex)
11. Share a good book. (Hare)
12. Some teenagers are very hip, pop, or op. They are swingers. (Hippo)
13. If you lean back, the chair will tip on you. (Pony)

Fish and Insects

1. There's a storekeeper whose initials are G. R. As shoppers go in and out, G. R. razzes them. (Grasshoppers)
2. Someone spilled ink. Now on Main and First, ink bugs everybody. (Stinkbugs)

---

[6] These sentences were done by Mike R., Jennifer Y., Holly B., Charles R., Francis D., Joan T., Susan P., Jim W., Betsy McL., David M., Clay J., Hugh McD., Denis F., Dena B., and Beth B.

3. A spoon was in the wrong drawer. (Asp)

4. A word Shakespeare's characters often use is "hark." (Shark)

5. Coffee lovers all over the world are switching to Yuban. (eel)

6. The days get hotter and more humid in the summer. (Otter)

7. He sat unable to think. (Tuna)

8. She put on her ring. (Herring)

9. He has a new carpet. (Carp)

10. Bob went out the door just before his mother rang the supper chime. (Perch)

11. I cut bugs in sections for biology. (Insect)

12. Did you flee cheerfully or sadly? (Leech)

13. The souffle and the rest of the dinner was good. (Flea)

Brand Names and Cartoon Characters

1. We have a visitor. (Avis)

2. The Monkees had over ten thousand letters. (Dover)

3. There is a Von's Shopping Bag Market in Pomona. (Avon)

4. As no Op yet has come to the art gallery, neither will people. (Snoopy)

5. We have the power to kill in us. (Linus)

6. France's ally was the United States. (Sally)

WORD PLAY

Game 6. Ounce, Dice, Trice is a delightful book, written by Alastair Reid and illustrated by Ben Shahn.[7] It should be a requisite in every classroom—for all kinds of groups, as long as everyone can see and hear and feel each magical word and drawing. The older children are fascinated by the brief stories, using "odd words, either forgotten or undiscovered, with which you can bamboozle almost anyone. They are arranged in Garlands which bring you always back to the beginning."[8] The students are able to weave their own fantastic creations. They willingly explore the pages of the dictionary to find words, a rare behavior for most children.

The younger children are equally intrigued. They giggle and repeat all the new sounds—music to their ears. Greedily, they want to hear more and invent more words for each category. "Novel counting systems," one category of words, provides the title of the book. Like the shepherds who

---

[7] Alastair Reid, *Ounce, Dice, Trice.*

[8] Reid, *Ounce, Dice, Trice*, p. 43.

concocted numbers to escape boredom, the children devise their own order. I think that this game alone would be a wonderful lesson as a change of pace in old or new math.

In a different vein, recent kindergarteners provided these words:

Heavy Words	*Light Words*
Blumenfeld	Air
Bubble	Many girls' names
Club	Michelle
Crocodile	Mississippi
Crud	Pencil sharpener
Flabbergast	Whistle
Garfunkel	
Grinch	
Hangnail	
Many boys' names	
Mud	
Numbskull	
Ooobleck	
Stupid	

The children were more interested in heavy words than light ones—rather like the struggle between good and evil! Just as the discussion turned to grumpy words, class time was up. On the run, a boy contributed a wonderful substitute word for bad moments: Stinkbug!

Days later, children were still using private words—like "mumbudget" to call for silence—or bringing in ones they had discovered. Exposure to special books like this creates an intimacy that no class should be without. (More about this point in the literature section.)

Game 7. Word play is the game I encountered in *Playboy* magazine, sometime in 1967. I tore the page from the issue and mounted it on colored paper to disguise its origins a little. Still somewhat fearful that the sixth-grade boys might know and reveal my source, I presented the idea to the class. As one of the older boys blurted out "I know where that comes from—" I held my breath. "—*Mad* magazine!" Everyone accepted the assignment immediately.

Some of the drawings reflect the influence of *Mad*; others are very original. In many cases they are done by the same children who needed to

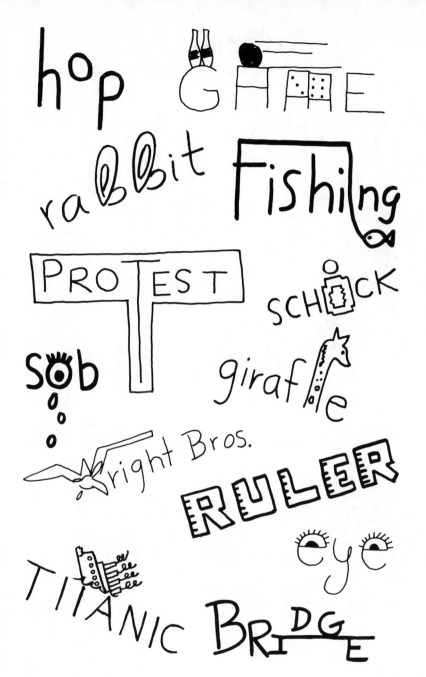

cat

CROAD ROSS

pARis

dover

GL⊕BE

Balloon

door

TAPE RECORDER

Flag

Lollipop

S⊤G⊙S

15 MI

⇒ARR⊚W

do a few familiar ones to practice. In the beginning it is unwise to hover over the children and inspect or criticize their work. I firmly believe in giving children time to warm up to the task. Once "revved up," they are delighted to show the teacher. When a child is floundering, his need is made obvious by his withdrawal. Then the adult can step in and clarify or ask a helpful, perhaps directing, question. An oversolicitous teacher inhibits the creative child and smothers the conformer. Such a pedagogue fosters no independence and inspires no creativity in the classroom.

PALINDROMES

Game 8. Palindromes are for sophisticated children of all ages. The younger children enjoy making a list of reversible words like *pop*, *Mom*, *Dad*, *Sis*. The older children can do that or can try to construct reversible sentences. Here are some tried and true palindromes for examples:

> Too hot to hoot.
> Pa's a sap.
> Rise to vote, sir.
> Step on no pets.
> No lemons, no melon.
> Too bad I hid a boot.
> 'Tis Ivan on a visit.
> Did Hannah see bees? Hannah did!
> Was it a rat I saw?
> Ten animals I slam in a net.
> Madam, I'm Adam.

Usually I give the class a sheet with these sentences on it and no definition. I then read it with the group and ask them what a palindrome is. They stare a while and figure it out. Climax! Some children try to make a palindrome. A few can.

Frequently children cannot meet this challenge, although they understand the principle. They can still have fun with the knowledge alone, if they can relax and attempt new ideas. Experiments do not always turn out, but they can be nevertheless fascinating. Teachers owe it to their children and themselves to stretch towards new concepts. The notion of reading the same idea forwards and backwards is novel and exciting to most children.

4. Serendipity   41

NAME GAMES; ACROSTICS

Game 9. With a little time, everyone can do an acrostic using his own name. It is a very good way to start the school year, because the focus is on individual identity, yet a group feeling begins to grow. I like to see the acrostics, which are boldly recopied on bright-colored construction paper, surround the classroom. The bulletin boards are unified and transformed to a brilliant dado.

There are numerous types of acrostics. Sometimes I demonstrate with my name, making a sentence based on current events:

Maury	Many
Really	Rulers
Steals	Say de
Gaining	Gaulle
Every	Evades
Other	Organizational
Run *vs.* the	Responsibility
Giants, his	Gluing
Enemy	Europe

No period after Mrs—no word begins with a period.

I try to keep all my words after the letters of my name. Some children cannot, because of their names or their ability. Since there is a variety of acrostics, I give the children lots of leeway to experiment. The only admonition is that their sentence must make sense. These two acrostics were done by sixth-graders:

Coughs
Are
Really
Old
Laughs,

Choked
Or
Left
Entirely
Noticeable.

Senator
Talmadge
Entertained
Vice Presidential
candidatEs
iN

Georgia
ThE
Interesting
Group
Enjoyed
Rum

Acrostics also tie in with social studies; in fact, a lesson on the Founding Fathers. This one, sent to Benjamin Franklin from Uncle Benjamin on July 15, 1710,[9] is the most complicated kind because it not only uses whole phrases or sentences for each letter in his name, but also rhymes:

Be to thy parents an Obedient son;
Each day let Duty constantly be done;
Never give Way to sloth or lust or pride
If free you'd be from Thousand Ills beside.
Above all Ills be sure Avoide the shelfe;
Mans Danger lyes in Satan, sin and selfe.
In vertue, Learning, Wisdome progress make.
Nere shrink at suffering for thy saviors sake;
Fraud and all Falshood in thy Dealings Flee;
Religious Always in thy station be;
Adore the Maker of thy Inward part:
Now's the Accepted time, Give him thy Heart.
Keep a Good Conscience, 'tis a constant Frind;
Like Judge and Witness This Thy Acts Attend.
In Heart with bended knee Alone Adore
None but the Three in One Forevermore.

Often I begin the session on acrostics by reading this one aloud to the class; the children follow along on their dittoed copies. Immediately they

---

[9] Leonard Labaree, ed., *The Autobiography of Benjamin Franklin.* p. 49.

note the "I" instead of a "J" and the "misspellings"! The experience becomes a lesson on typography and spelling, as well as on acrostics.

Children do not realize the changes in the English language since the colonies became a country. It amazes them to know that the awesome subject, Correct Spelling, has not always been the same. They are very attentive during sessions which involve primary-source reading. As long as they can see and hear the "old fashioned" writing, they enjoy the contact with the past.

NAME GAMES: ANAGRAMS

Game 10. There are always several children who cannot get enough of name play. For them, I suggest anagrams. This activity is too strict a discipline for general classroom use. A person has to be very adept to manipulate only the letters of his name into a statement. He has to have a crossword-puzzle mentality to succeed. Alas, I am not such a person. My husband is, and claims that the sentences or phrases derived from a person's name are as significant as his horoscope—if at all!

"Characteristic initials" is another method that everyone could do for himself or someone famous. (It might get too vindictive if applied to other children.) A person's initials must be the initials of a phrase that describes him. For example[10]: Florence Nightingale was a Famous Nurse; Edgar Allan Poe, an Early American Poet; Chiang Kai-shek, China's Kingpin. For the youngest children, the book *My Name Is.*[11] is useful and fun.

NAME GAMES: ELECTION PREDICTIONS

Game 11. The fascination with names becomes public during presidential elections—at least it spreads to the domain of the classroom. Children make campaign slogans, displaying buttons with all of their parents' political preferences. The room teeters with the unbalanced weight of partisanship. If overt activities are suppressed, the campaign moves underground to the playground, the cafeteria, the washrooms, wherever adults do not look too closely.

I have found one way for the teacher to participate and yet remain nonpartisan. With help from a word wizard like Dmitri Borgmann, he can

[10] Dmitri Borgmann, *Language on Vacation.*
[11] Louise Baker Muehl, *My Name Is.*

PRESIDENTIAL ELECTION PREDICTION

1. Historically the oldest one: Vote goes to the candidate with the longer name. Wrong only twice, 1880-1960.

2. Double letters. Never wrong, 1896-1960.

3. Taller candidates. Wrong only twice, 1888-1960.

4. Add up sum. of year. ODD year = Democratic. EVEN year = Republican. 100% accuracy from 1896 to 1936; 1940 to 1960, the situation was reversed.

Play around with this list and the election results tonight for Senate, State offices, and even Sycamore School.

CANDIDATES

Year (odd-even)	Winner (no. of letters, height for both male opponents)	Loser
1880	Garfield (8)	Hancock (7)
1884	Cleveland (9)	Blaine (6)
1888	Harrison (8) 5'6"	Cleveland (9) 5'11"
1892	Cleveland (9) 5'11"	Harrison (8) 5'6"
1896 Even-R	William McKinley (8) 5'10"	Bryan (5) 5'10"
1900 Even-R	Same	Same
1904 Even-R	Roosevelt (9) 5'10"	Parker (6) 5'9"
1908 Even-R	William Taft (4) 6'0"	Bryan (5) 5'10"
1912 Odd-D	Woodrow Wilson (6) 5'11"	Taft (4) 5'10½"
1916 Odd-D	Same	Hughes (6) 5'10"
1920 Even-R	Warren Harding (7) 6'0"	Cox (3) 5'10"
1924 Even-R	Coolidge (8) 5'10"	Davis (5) 5'9½"
1928 Even-R	Hoover (6) 6'0"	Smith (5) 5'11"
1932 Odd-D	Roosevelt (9) 6'2"	Hoover (6) 6'0"
1936 Odd-D	Same	Landon (6) 5'11"
1940 Even-D	Same	Willkie (7) 6'2½"
1944 Even-D	Same	Dewey (5) 5'8"
1948 Even-D	Harry Truman (6) 5'9"	Same
1952 Odd-R	D. D. Eisenhower (10) 5'10½"	Stevenson (9) 5'10"
1956 Odd-R	Same	Same
1960 Even-D	Kennedy (7) 6'0"	Nixon (5) 5'11"

4. Serendipity

channel the students' enthusiasm and energies in new directions. "The Presidency: Study in Depth," Chapter 9 from *Language on Vacation*,[12] provides all kinds of intriguing possibilities. Intact, it is almost a complete unit for the social studies. Fragments from it serve as enrichment.

One section called "Election Predictions" amazed me, so I consolidated the facts onto a ditto. Since it was an off-year with "little elections," as the children decreed, I had to make some adjustments.

The children and their parents were intrigued and entertained by this assignment. Again they spent the evening by the television set, testing the hypotheses. (Mr. Borgmann, we love you. One boy, however, would like to go down on record for asking "Why is William Howard Taft an inch and a half shorter in 1912 than in 1908? Was the presidency that difficult?")

THE CURRENT SCENE

Game 12. Button designing has come into vogue with the manufacture of blank buttons which the purchaser completes. One of the boys in a recent class enameled over an old button and painted in a peace symbol to be more contemporary. Right there he had a good and cheap idea for an art lesson in political science: Let the children design their own campaign buttons for the election. The apolitical could make a cultural button—like "Pooh loves you" or psychedelia.

The children also had a "chalk-in" on large rolls of butcher paper rather than pavement (so that the teacher could roll it up quickly if the administration protested!) It was inspired by news coverage of an art show in Watts. The results were beautiful—bold designs in wild colors, hiding words like Mellow Yellow, Weirdo, Jefferson Airplane, LSD. They were far more Art Nouveau than "tuned out." These children of a conservative, with a small "c," community gleefully played hippies for an afternoon of art in the sun. Their rebellion was joyful and sweet.

I would never deprive children of language experiences from the contemporary interests, even fads. To do so would sap their vitality and betray their trust in me, but more important, in expression. The teacher needs to be concerned with communication, genuine and experimental. The reactions of the community are secondary and usually sympathetic if there is a strong rationale.

Language is taught too haphazardly. Teachers do not think out their

[12] Borgmann, pp. 261-282.

"approach." They mimic others. The program ends up as space filler—mere assorted exercises with rigid requirements. The children subjected to these do not learn to write or to think. Once a teacher thinks out his approach in terms of philosophy rather than commas, he can afford to be more open-ended. He knows the importance of experimentation, of disregarding rules occasionally to really understand them. Most children recognize this philosophy not as permissiveness but as commitment. Once the children understand, their parents do, too. I try to get both sympathetic and antagonistic parents to participate on a regular basis in the program. It is amazing how much more people are helped to comprehend by doing.

EQUIVOQUES

Game 13. Equivoques appeal to the spy in everyone. They are the artful product of inscrutability. Children snap them up, because equivoques come across like James Bond and provide outlets for extreme emotions. Teachers can use them not only for therapeutic value, but also for instructional worth and fun.

THE WAR OF INDEPENDENCE

Procedure:

(1) Choose one fiction book from the period of the Revolutionary War. (Johnny Tremain, Bells of Freedom, Treegate's Raiders, or any other book by Wibberly are a few examples.)

(2) Read it carefully and begin to think about these issues:

   a. Details of life at that time

      For example, do they have things we do not use today? Do they do things we would not?

   b. Details of the struggle

      What famous persons or battles are mentioned?

(3) Decide how true the whole story seems to you. Do you have any evidence?

Format: two to three pages on white lined paper

   You may write your essay in any way that is clear to you and the reader. If your book provokes other questions, feel free to discuss them.

A Triple Platform

''Among the memorials of the sectional conflict of 1861-1865, is an American platform arranged to suit all parties. The first column is the Secession; the second, the Aboliton platform; and the whole, read together, is the Democratic platform:''

Hurrah for	The Old Union
Secession	Is a curse
We fight for	The Constitution
The Confederacy	Is a league with hell
We love	Free speech
The rebellion	Is treason
We glory in	A Free Press
Separation	Will not be tolerated
We fight not for	The negro's freedom
Reconstruction	Must be obtained
We must succeed	At every hazard
The Union	We love
We love not	The negro
We never said	Let the Union slide
We want	The Union as it was
Foreign intervention	Is played out
We cherish	The old flag
The stars and bars	Is a flaunting lie
We venerate	The habeas corpus
Southern chivalry	Is hateful
Death to	Jeff Davis
Abe Lincoln	Isn't the Government
Down with	Mob law
Law and order	Shall triumph.

Equivoques, literally *double meanings*, tie in with the social studies. The examples from the Revolutionary and Civil War periods were discovered in *Oddities and Curiosities of Words and Literature*,[13] an indispensable Dover paperback. I read several kinds of equivoques to the class, who follow along on the usual ditto, before giving them writing paper. They admire the antique craftsmanship of rhyme and vocabulary.

The most typical equivoques hide the real meaning in alternate lines. The Bombaugh book gives the examples of a love letter and a letter by a disenchanted bride. Neither gem would be appropriate for use in the elementary schools, so the children are told about writing letters with the hidden meaning on every other line. As a whole, the equivoque should have a meaning opposite from the one intended. The children come up with some excellent devices.

> My brother is
> far from being
> a twerp, pipsqueak, whimp.
> Andy is so sweet
> He thinks only of
> avoiding at all times
> biting, kicking and pulling hair.
> I love his little friends.
> His playmates are just like him.
>
> [Randy F., age 10]

The Rolling Stones are
A group of the neatest singers. Some people say the Beatles are
the dumbest singers around.
I don't like them to think this about the R.S. I won't live to the day
they sing off tune. And should
I, I would be very sad. I never thought that they should
not be allowed in the singing world.
I wish that I could hear them.
I think that they should go
on singing trips always and not go
back to England and forget
about us in America. I will never forget
the whole thing!

[Sue Belle S., age 11]

[13] C. C. Bombaugh, *Oddities and Curiosities of Words and Literature*, pp. 67-69.

4. Serendipity

THE CLASSROOM CALENDAR

A calendar in the classroom can do more than note holidays—it can also organize part of a language program. There are many anniversaries of events and birthdays of notables, besides those of the students. The facts themselves, like good books, often suggest an assignment or an enrichment activity.

Here are a few dates for each month of the school year which have such possibilities:

September 2. Gregorian calendar adopted by Great Britain and colonies in 1752. Next day was September 14, dropping eleven days overnight. This jump makes thorough historians cite important dates as follows: George Washington's birthday, February 22 (February 11 O.S.)

September 4. First transcontinental television broadcast, 1951.

September 9. "United States" (rather than United Colonies) becomes official name, 1776.

October 4. Sputnik, first man-made satellite, 1957.

October 19. Earl of Sandwich invented the sandwich, 1744.

November 12. Elizabeth Cady Stanton born, 1816.

November 17. Suez Canal opened, 1879.

December 16. Boston Tea Party, 1773.

January 6. Carl Sandburg born, 1875.

January 18. A. A. Milne born, 1882.

January 27. Lewis Carroll born, 1832.

February 20. First manned orbital space flight for United States by John Glenn, 1962.

March 10. First sentence spoken over telephone, 1876.

March 21. Johann Sebastian Bach born, 1685.

March 26. Robert Frost born, 1874.

April 18. Paul Revere's ride, 1775.

April 23. William Shakespeare allegedly born, 1564.

May 6. Peter Minuit bought Manhattan from the Indians, 1626.

May 21. First solo Atlantic flights: Charles Lindbergh, 1927; Amelia Earhart, 1932.

May 23. First automobile trip across the United States, San Francisco to New York, from May 23 to August 1, 1903.

There are a number of other sources for intriguing dates. A good public library will be stocked with such references as these:

Douglas, George. *American Book of Days*, New York, H. W. Winston Co., 1948.

Hazeltine, Mary. *Anniversaries and Holidays*, Chicago, American Library Association, 1928.

Hutchinson, Ruth, and Ruth Adams. *Every Day's a Holiday*, New York, Harper and Bros., 1951.

Schoyer, Will. *Schoyer's Vital Anniversaries of the Known World* (annual), Pittsburgh, Will Schoyer and Co.

The *World Almanac* and *Guinness Book of World Records* are also extremely helpful for vital statistics. Local radio stations and newspapers use fillers with such facts. A keen-eared, sharp-eyed teacher can pick up information on the way to work. *The Calendar*, issued quarterly by the Children's Book Council, is discussed on page 70, in Chapter Six.

The teacher does not need to fill in every date, unless he is compulsive. The children will find some of their own to add.

4. Serendipity   51

chapter five

SKILLS

A chapter on skills, following the experiences of serendipity, is not a cold shower and flagellation after a sauna bath. In my view "skills" is a division purely for convenience. It is artificial, as indeed are all the divisions. Knowledge cannot be put in discrete categories. The effort to make such categories is one of the problems of education today. From kindergarten on, administrators worry about distribution requirements, whether they are counting hours allocated to physical education and reading or units towards a major and minor. The time has passed for any uniformly graded, up tight, standardized system. With machines to do most work, human uniformity is no longer necessary. Considering the diversity of leisure, rather than work, it is no longer desirable.

In general, skills are an extension of the thinking process—the more clearly a person can think, the better he can communicate by written or spoken word. (It always used to infuriate me when a seventh-grade teacher insisted, "Mary, if you knew the answer, you could state it. There is no such thing as knowing it and not being able to put it in words." Until recently I had written her off as a New England schoolmarm!)

SPELLING

To me, skills such as punctuation are symptomatic of a person's verbal development. As signals they are important; as pressing issues, they are not. Therefore, the writing of each child is treated individually. I read every paper and write specific comments on content and style. I also list all the spelling words missed. In general, the errors I find during the week, *except* in creative writing, become the basis of the child's spelling program. He uses them in writing spelling sentences and studies them for a weekly review. This method seems preferable to the use of state texts which do not answer individual needs.

Perhaps I should clarify the exclusion of words missed in creative writing. I take the view that if a child is a poor speller, he is most likely a reluctant writer. He does not like to put his thoughts down on paper. A private spelling list based on his mistakes only penalizes him. It is important to "objectify" his spelling words. Thus, in my class, he uses a Dolch list of basic English words.

This program works quite well. The best spellers or those who consult the dictionary are rewarded by getting fewer words to study. The poorest spellers have their own tutorial with parents and college students, rather than being penalized in their struggles with written work. (Once I gave a list of thirty-seven pairs of words to the whole group. It consisted of the names of all the children in the class. That would certainly be a good way to start in September. I did it toward the end of the year in desperation, as children were still misspelling the names of their classmates and even their best friends!)

Usually the children come together for a spelling program only at one point. Once a year the class spends a few weeks on S.R.A. kits[1] to be exposed to spelling concepts. At that, the system is individualized; each student works on a track suitable to his spelling achievement. The work can degenerate into blind routine, where clerical accomplishments outweigh phonic development. Therefore, I place a time limit of a month on the use of such programmed material.

---

[1] *Spelling Word Power Laboratory* (grades 4-7), developed by Dr. Don H. Parker for Science Research Associates, 259 East Erie Street, Chicago, Illinois 60611.

This procedure seems lengthy, and it is overwhelming at times, especially since I like to make my comments promptly. However, I feel it helps my teaching because of the closer contact with the child. The comments also lighten my preparation for the long narrative evaluation twice a year. (A standard report card with grades would be inconsistent with the program of individualization.)

A friend recently sent me a game which would be excellent for spelling and vocabulary building, even using the dictionary. "Perquackey"[2] got her through tedious moments of law school in New Haven. A speedy relative of "Scrabble," using lettered dice to spell words within a three-minute period, it is addictive and social, allowing any number of participants. Several sets, in addition to chess and checkers, should stimulate a lot of thinking during periods of independent activity. I think good games, including commercial ones, are legitimate and necessary additions to the curriculum.

CAPITALIZATION

Occasionally I give the whole class an assignment that could be construed as a skill builder. I try to cover the vitamin with sugar coating. For instance, "The Story of Esaw Wood" is the perfect foil for a lesson on capitalization. The children, each armed with a ditto lacking all capital letters, begin to see the light about the importance of that convention. There is no need for preaching at all.

"Esaw," dizzying though it be, is a good introduction to further work on capitalization. The children bring in their own rules for usage and compile a list of situations where capital letters are required. There is a lively discussion with far more involvement and sophistication than would have emerged from a cold list in a grammar book.

DICTATION

For a skill like dictation, which is used heavily for instruction in foreign languages, a teacher should find intriguing passages from good books. Limited use of dictated passages in the native tongue is good practice for listening to details and for spelling. It is a waste of time to practice on

---

[2] "Perquackey," a product of Lakeside Toys, Minneapolis, Minnesota, is readily available in stationery and toy stores.

the story of esaw wood

esaw wood sawed wood.

esaw wood would saw wood.

all the wood esaw wood saw esaw wood would saw. in other words, all the wood esaw saw to saw esaw sought to saw. oh, the wood wood would saw! and oh, the wood-saw with which wood would saw wood!

but one day wood's wood-saw would saw no wood, and thus the wood wood sawed was not the wood wood would saw if wood's wood-saw would saw wood.

in fact, of all the wood-saws wood ever saw saw wood wood never saw a wood-saw that would saw wood as the wood-saw wood saw saw wood would saw wood, and i never saw a wood-saw that would saw as the wood-saw wood saw would saw until i saw esaw wood saw with the wood-saw wood saw saw wood.

From C. C. Bombaugh, Oddities and Curiosities of Words and Litera-ture, edited and annotated by Martin Gardner. Dover Publications, Inc., New York, 1961. Reprinted through the permission of the publisher. Originally published in 1896 as Gleanings for the Curious. (An abbre-viated version.)

"spelling stories" written by someone in class, when selections such as "The Cockroach" from *Creatures of Darkness*[3] are readily available:

"The common house roach is a scuttling, scurrying dirty yellow crea-ture that feeds on floor crumbs in dark kitchens and carouses in damp bathrooms. The nicest thing about it is its antennae, which have about eighty joints."

Haunting pen-and-ink studies accompany other selections in this book about bedbugs, owls, bats, wolves, and their kind. The boys and girls enjoy thoroughly these examples of excellent writing, perfect blends of scientific observation and poetic statement.

[3] Esther and Leonard Baskin, *Creatures of Darkness.*

5. Skills

SUMMARIES AND OUTLINES

Summaries and outlines are useful techniques to learn. Summaries can be very boring, if the student is not interested in the subject he is covering. For practice, I ask the children to listen to a half-hour program of their choice on television or radio, then hand in synopses. Those I receive are usually well-written. The boys do a particularly ardent job during the baseball season, reporting many innings of action. Outlines can be treated in a similar manner. The biggest mistake a teacher can make is to impose a system of organization upon anyone. An adult can suggest or show the standard outline, composed of I, A, 1, a, 1), a) *ad nauseam.* However, he must allow each child to develop his own meaningful order, over the years if necessary, as adults do. How many grownups take notes in the manner prescribed by so many teachers? Clarity is the issue, not compulsion.

I tend to favor assignments which include pooling information from individuals in the class. The results are not only personal, but also impressive. This technique also saves the teacher some time, which can be spent elsewhere.

Before itemizing such assignments, I had better remind the reader that this book is a concentration of ideas which have worked for me. A number of them involve outside work. Therefore, I do not recommend compressing the following assignments into one school year. The level of pupil enthusiasm is directly proportional to the teacher's selectivity. If it is deficient, he will have a bunch of cynical, overworked children with a show-me attitude.

TIMELINES

A personal timeline is another good way to start the school year. Composing one is a definable skill with some promise of deeper knowledge. The child marks off his lifespan on a ruled, horizontal line, midway down a large sheet of paper. Above the line he writes events which have happened in his own life, to him and to his family. Below the line he enters world events—sports, science, politics, anything. Parents and encyclopedias or almanacs are preferred resources to find something noteworthy for every year. It is interesting rather than overwhelming for the children, if the teacher cares to use his own timeline as a guide. Somehow the gesture of baring one's age and activities—to a certain extent—is intimate and immediate, almost like saying "Let's be friends."

DICTIONARIES

Children in love with words will read any dictionary as a pastime. However, the right set of dictionaries can enrich a language program, rather than merely exist on the sidelines. In particular, the *Oxford Universal Dictionary on Historical Principles*[4] can win the interest of children who never use reference books, as well as excite the *aficionados*, because it includes fascinating details. Besides the standard pronunciation, etymology, and definition, the dictionary offers the chronology of each word. Children can see when a word came into use and how it has changed since its earliest known occurrence. An example of each change is given, using quotations from literature and historic figures.

WORDS' WORTH

1. Use a dictionary to try to find out where and when these words entered the English language:

gnu, trek, punch, luftwaffe, dungaree, kindergarten, boycott,

grenade, alligator, chocolate, carnival, madrigal, yacht.

2. What other words do you know from foreign languages that we commonly use?

3. These words have been in the English language for several hundred years. However, their meaning has changed since they were first used. What are the new and old definitions?

fancy, wit, with, speedy, dizzy, starve, knave, shall, bury, owe.

---

[4] No revised edition of this dictionary, at least with this title, is listed in the current catalog of the Oxford University Press. A dictionary much like it, which can be obtained in the 1970s, appears to be *The Shorter Oxford English Dictionary on Historical Principles*, prepared by William Little, H. W. Fowler, J. Coulson, rev. and ed. by Charles Talbot Onions, 3rd ed., 1944, reprinted with revised addenda 1955, and corrections, 1962. This dictionary, in various bindings, was priced in the 1968 Oxford catalog at $30 to $37.25. Good used copies sell for $10 to $15. If your school is wealthy, maybe you can requisition *The Oxford English Dictionary* (13 volumes; $300). You might prefer to supplement your present dictionaries with *The Oxford Dictionary of English Etymology*, ed. C. T. Onions and others, 1966. (Price $16.50 in 1968.)

So that children would become familiar with the use of the dictionary, I gave them an assignment.[5] These three questions alone provide the basis for a unit on word origins or parallel a study of immigration in social studies. In either case, the topic lends itself to several weeks of interesting inquiry.

Antonyms also exercise dictionary skills. One of the easiest ways to play around with the concept is "Backward Advertising." (The teacher can also highlight a particular part of speech, killing two birds if he wants.) The children bring in ads from magazines and convert key words to their opposites. They cannot use negatives. It is a good idea to use scratch paper first and then glue a bright patch with the antonym over the old word, like a collage.

BIBLIOGRAPHIES

I am more fiendish about the use of bibliographies than dictionaries, perhaps because a basic issue seems to be at stake. Throughout a child's schooling, he is tempted by the easy knowledge in the *World Book* and other encyclopedias. He turns in assignments, literally lifted from those volumes. If he copies an article out for me, word for word, I am a bit disappointed but not angry *if*—if he cites his source. Too often teachers require rephrasing "in your own words" and accept the product without attribution, wasting time as well as missing the whole idea. It is integrity represented by the awareness of the source, not the modified plagiarism, that is crucial. Children must know the places where they find information, so that they can defend or question the facts. Children must not become hack writers or unimaginative editors. Therefore, a simple bibliography stating author and title at the end of any paper is important.

ANTHOLOGIES

For these reasons I give the children compilation tasks several times a year. Sometimes they collect poems for an anthology on a specific subject like the moon, dedicated to their science teacher. The types of poems that the children bring in are very revealing. The selected poems indicate quite a bit about the reading habits of their families, since most of the children

---

[5] The assignment reflects suggestions in *The Tree of Language*, by Helene and Charlton Laird. This book is rich with other provocative material geared directly to classroom use.

try to do their assignments at home rather than at the library. Children submit poems by major bards like Shelley, Wordsworth, Eliot, and Frost, as well as examples by lesser stars like Teasdale, Lindsay, Sidney, Stevenson, and Farjeon. The anthology is published with the title and the poet's name in the heading and the child's name at the end of each selection. This pattern sinks in, as the students quietly read the poems, apparently satisfied by their new roles of scholarship. I would hate to see the children succumb to chronic pedantry. However, it is important for them to appreciate the meaning of originality. This approach is one of the avenues toward realization.

The children perform a similar task during their study of the westward movement of the United States. Using anthologies of American folk tales, they choose a favorite legendary hero or heroine. They are asked to write about one event in his life, sticking as close to the "truth" as possible. (They discover the truth is hard to find, since different storytellers exaggerate the "facts." Then they use their favorite version.) The tales center on Paul Bunyan, Pecos Bill, Johnny Appleseed, Davy Crockett, Mike Fink, Annie Christmas, Kemp Morgan, Febold Feboldson, John Henry. Surprisingly, the anecdotes have not yet overlapped.

Later, when a book is dittoed and assembled, the class discusses the folk hero and his place in history. Walter Blair's *Tall Tale America*[6] is good preparation. It is worth glancing at the book, if only for its humorous map, locating some of the heroes. A lesson in geography would be most enjoyable with whimsical notes like "Since this map was made, some of these fellows may have moved," or "Warning: This map is not recommended by the Coast and Geodetic Survey."

In *A Nation of Immigrants*, President Kennedy listed almost a page of "American" foods that have immigrated along with the books from foreign countries. Just reading the catalogue made the class hungry and ready to write poems on food, which accompanied gourmet recipes later brought from home. The children became junior Walt Whitmans and Carl Sandburgs of cuisine.[7] Their collection, called *The Melting Pot*, was presented to eager parents on Mother's Day, a holiday which the children insistently celebrate.

An assignment that everyone enjoys was concocted on the spur of the

---

[6] Walter Blair, *Tall Tale America*.

[7] See Rose Agree, ed., *How to Eat a Poem and Other Morsels: Food Poems for Children*.

moment, en route to the public library on a Friday the thirteenth. At the time the class was studying mythology and archeology, somehow lovely topics for January. Using the *Encyclopedia of Superstitions*,[8] another book that should be in every school library, the children each list five superstitions that intrigue them. They are asked to concentrate on one of them: "When was it popular?" "Is it still believed?" "Why do you think it is (was) believed?"

The variety of responses is exciting, at times highly amusing. I offer some abbreviated notes from the discussion which turned up over sixty superstitions, many new to the class.

Myth and Superstition

Myth is a story, explaining how things came to be. It answers questions.

Superstition is a belief, a warning, a coincidence. See the following examples:

1. Death watch beetle = death to someone in the house.
2. Drop dishrag or silverware = unexpected guests.
3. [Censored!]
4. $ in shoe leads to more $.
5. Full moon, time of going crazy or turning into werewolf.
6. Bat flying out of cave early signifies fine day.
7. Light hair = fickle girls; dark hair = sincere, healthier girls; red hair = unstable, quick-tempered girls.
9. Lick a lizard to cure sickness.
11. Roast a mouse and eat it to cure whooping cough.
17. Horse hair left in water turns into eels.
18. Change in rhythm of clock's ticking = death.
19. Rice at weddings keeps away evil.
20. Witches travel in empty egg shells and cause shipwrecks.
21. Last drink on New Year's Eve = good luck.
27. Drop glove, don't pick it up. Bad luck.
30. Anything with number five like a hand protects people from the evil eye.
32. Hangman's rope cures headaches.
33. Sleep on right side = long life, left side = twenty years.
38. Always stir batter in the same direction. (Italy)
47. Evil spirit travels in straight line, so crooked bridges in Japan.
48. Chinese roofs curved to catch evil spirits.
61. For each falling autumn leaf you catch, you receive a happy month.

[8]E. and M. A. Radford, *Encyclopedia of Superstitions.*

Note three, regretfully censored in the example, was a high point in the discussion. A delightful and unforgettable boy, known for his perceptive comments, raised his hand. He contributed shyly but deliberately, "A mole on the left booby indicates . . ." He never finished the sentence above the roar of the crowd. What a researcher!

This adventure turned into an entertaining art lesson. When the children received their copies of the discussion notes, they each chose a superstition to illustrate. As usual, the format was large, the colors bold. The products which ran around the top of the blackboards leaped out at the beholder and pulled him into the eccentric classroom.

LETTERS

Another skill, letter writing, can be fun. After all, good letters are imaginative, full of interesting details. Letters are the perfect vehicle to exercise viewpoint. A traveler from another place or era writes home about his impressions. Or the other way around, natives write to a traveler. The children collected letters, pictures, and puzzles for a departing exchange student and bound them into a book, limited edition of one. A letter shown here is typical of the warm, natural style that most of the children mastered.

Room 11, Sycamore School
Claremont, California
January 10, 1965

Dear Atsuko,

I hope you enjoyed your visit to the U.S.A. Our class has enjoyed having you. It is too bad you did not get to visit the other states. California is a good state, but Oregon and Washington have more state and national parks and beaches. If you ever get a chance to come back, try to go to those two states. You should try to go to Disneyland. It is a blast.

I hope you and your brother can skateboard real well when you get home to Japan.

Have a safe trip home.

Your friend,

[Howie U., age 11]

Letters are exciting contacts with famous people. I read the children Bill Adler's *Love Letters to the Beatles*, mainly because they knew and loved the letters. They really didn't need any motivation and they didn't fall into the trap of being glib, as I had feared from Adler's collection. Afterward, the children wrote to "someone they admired from a distance." One month later, replies began to trickle in from all over the world. It was interesting to note which celebrities answered their mail personally rather than by form letters and postcards, and which people answered promptly. Writers and artists, such as Louise Fitzhugh, Roald Dahl, Charles Schulz, and Igor Stravinsky seemed to need and appreciate the children's attention. In contrast, figures in the fickle limelight were less sympathetic or more bogged down by mail. There were no responses at year's end from the Smothers Brothers, the Beatles, or Don Drysdale.

Besides headings, punctuation, and other mechanics, the children learned an unspoken lesson from this assignment. They knew the disappointment of receiving a mass-produced letter or none at all, and the joy of a delightful, personal contact with someone who cared.

INTRODUCTORY SENTENCES

I approach the whole business of the introductory sentence as a journalist with his 5 *W*'s. Equipped with *who*, *what*, *when*, *why*, and *where*, the children feel prepared to start putting their thoughts down on paper. They do not falter, as they did in the past before being furnished the "formula."

However, to avoid churning out petty reporters, I begin with a quest for good first sentences from favorite books. The assignment really serves two purposes: the children must decide what books they like best and they must locate a good opening passage. The two do not always occur together. The quality of the selections is usually astounding. One year the class returned with excerpts from J. B. Tolkien, Mark Twain, Lewis Carroll, E. B. White, Louise Fitzhugh, Sally Carrighar, Herman Melville, A. A. Milne, C. S. Lewis, Beverly Cleary, Thornton Wilder, Jules Verne, Madeleine L'Engle, Robert Louis Stevenson, Armstrong Sperry, and Ian Fleming. (It would have taken a hard day's night for me to assemble such excellent examples.)

Using the dittoed sentences *with their sources*, the class discusses the contents. Without teacher intervention, they are able to identify the ingredients and decide how much information is in the sentence. After they survey the scene, I then mention the journalistic conventions of the 5 *W*'s and even the inverted triangle. (The 5 *W*'s are at the broad top; the story dwindles down to trivia at the bottom point. Thus, the reader or editor can lop off the end of an article to save time or space.) The essential of the approach is to let the children feel they have discovered the key. A teacher should restrain himself until the main points have come across.

QUOTATION MARKS–DIALOGUE

Quotation marks are discouraging, to teach and to learn. Yet they set in motion a month-long project which was engrossing and entertaining–a happy product of despair. I started by trying to reduce the quotation system to a formula or two, which I shared with the class:

(1) —— said, "——."

(2) "——?" asked ——.

Then I assigned the children two brief conversations, one from real life at school or at home and one from a television program. They were to act as observers, mere recorders, rather than participants. The conversations were brought in the next day and posted on blackboards for correction and approval by the class. (No ditto this time!)

QUOTATION MARKS–PUPPETS

The initial puppet assignment was a "jabberwocky," a creature drawn with felt-tip pens on the hand. (The side or back of the hand has the face; a mouth is formed by the index finger and thumb.) The children had one practice session with the instant puppets and dialogue. They rehearsed privately and wrote down their conversations, which could be old jokes like a vaudeville routine, new material, or a news interview.

For several days the class enjoyed a parade of talent. The jabberwockies not only talked but also whistled, croaked, chewed gum, smoked cigarettes, and stuck out tongues (on the ends of pencils). The television commercials, using a similar gimmick to advertise tissue paper, could have learned a few things from the amateurs. The jabberwockies were so successful that they spread throughout the school to all ages and both sexes.

At the beginning of the next phase, I read aloud skits from *Punch and Judy*, a handsome book by Ed Emberly. The children loved the outrageous slapstick, howling at the puppets' antics. They also learned conventions of writing scripts for plays, like stage directions and the use of colons rather than quotation marks. They were ready to write plays on their own or to collaborate in teams when I distributed the assignment sheets.

The children had three weeks to write, cast, and produce their plays.

```
ASSIGNMENT: PLAY

At least three pages on white lined paper.

Use either dialogue form--

          Punch: Judy, come here!

or direct quotations--

          Punch says, ''Judy, come here!''

You may write three short skits that are related, like Punch and
Judy, or

You may write an original play or choose a retelling of a familiar
story, even lip-synch.

     Please be sure your play has:

(1) a strong beginning which includes details explaining the 5 W's--
what, which, when, why, where;

(2) a strong middle which doesn't drag; and

(3) a satisfying end, which solves the ''dilemma.''
```

Somehow they juggled all three roles simultaneously during afternoons of independent reading and/or puppetry. It was a lovely, relaxed spring.

The puppets themselves were no problem. During the previous year, most of the children had worked with papier maché and burlap stitchery. They knew how to mold a head with exaggerated features, to thread a needle, and to work with fabric. (For some reason, the boys always sewed with a single thread. While they stitched neatly, the piece fell apart much easier than the girls' things which were tenaciously sewn. Nonetheless, the boys were enthusiastic and proud of their handiwork.) I will never forget the look on the face of a visitor who surveyed the scene of children sewing intently. The relative quiet of the class was shattered by a definite Tom Sawyer type, roaring, "Who took my needle?!!!

The children were encouraged to invent puppets, using new techniques. Some painted tennis balls for heads; others used detergent bottles for bodies. A very simple puppet is plausible so long as some part of it moves.

Body, arms, legs, head—any one or all together can do effective and expressive acting. Moving mouths make dialogue convincing, whether words are spoken by the child-manipulator himself or played from a record or tape with "lip" synchronization. A rubber ball, split and hinged, is a lifelike speaker. It can be fastened to a "body" painted on a flat piece of cardboard and can be opened and closed by various kinds of concealed handles.

101 Hand Puppets[9] has some excellent ideas for "pop puppets": (1) A quartet, composed of four split-rubber-ball heads fixed in a row on a painted frame. The mouths move on a long single hinge, simultaneously gaping and closing—perfect for a chorus. (2) A Martian, its head made from a toy rocket ship. A hose runs unseen through the body and up to the hatch on top of the head for blowing bubbles. (3) A two-hand-puppet dachshund, tail wagged by one hand, head moved by the other. The two parts of the dog are linked by a Slinky[10] covered with brown velvet.

Watching the productions, I realized that another "must" for the model classroom is a puppet stage: at least a table turned on its side or a big corrugated-board box. Better still would be a large wooden stage front with hinges to facilitate moving and folding away for storage. Puppetry can certainly revitalize a flagging language and art program. Building on these experiences, the class can experiment with marionettes, which are more complicated. If they do not get an opportunity in elementary school, the children will probably never know the thrill of working with their hands and brains in this delightful way.

[9] Richard Cummings, *101 Hand Puppets: a Guide for Puppeteers of All Ages.*

[10] Slinky, a flexible metal coil, is manufactured by James Industries, Hollidaysburg, Pennsylvania.

part two

LITERATURE

chapter six

READING ALOUD TO CHILDREN

BACKGROUND

Literature plays a special role in the classroom. It is the great unifier. Well-chosen books express difficult ideas and emotions, which involve the children immediately. As the year progresses, the class builds up a large backlog of literary experiences that are as meaningful as day-to-day happenings.

In fact, literature in some form is a daily event. The phrase "in some form" should be stressed, because literature is multifaceted. I try to approach it always from different angles of reading, writing, and art. I do not want "literature" to become a neat, predictable subject that would betray the beauty and variety of books. Above all, I try to avoid the typical feedback—a standard book report. The children rapidly develop an immunity to style, characterization, and other artistic glories when forced into traditional retellings of the plot. Too many teachers have archaic ideas about story structure. They require children to respond in a set pattern which takes a sledge hammer to undo in high school. Delaying the natural reactions to a book and denying insights on the grounds of "immaturity" are pedagogical crimes, punishable by at least one course in contemporary American literature or Joyce, Yeats, Eliot. Who is old enough—or too old—to appreciate a good book? As C. S. Lewis said, "No book is really worth reading at the age of ten which is not equally (and often far more) worth reading at the age of fifty."[1]

The book population on the juvenile shelves has been exploding. The huge realm of children's books is at once bewildering and exciting. Authors explore many new directions, charting reactions that are much more honest than those in the sweet, condescending books of the past. It is a large task, often demanding a book a night, for a teacher to catch up with only the exceptional books written since his childhood. The rewards are great, because another dimension of teaching unfolds.

PREPARATION

There are several ways to begin a crash program of reading. If the adult does not feel confident about his ability to "divine" significant books, he can consult a list of the Newbery and Caldecott Awards, a librarian, or a child who is a dedicated reader. (It is wonderful to have book finders in the class—children who will loan their own copies of books to convert the teacher.) *The Calendar*, a tiny quarterly issued by the Children's Book Council[2] is packed with recommendations based on a theme and with information about book awards, prizes, free materials and publications, and important dates to observe in the classroom. Some bookstores give away catalogues which neatly divide recent books into categories by age and subject with ratings by the American Library Association. Each year the A.L.A. also selects Notable Books. Their list is usually available at the public library.

The Children's Book Center of the Claremont Graduate School publishes an annual, which honors selected authors and reviews books of "compelling interest." *According To Us* appears every February at the

---

[1] C. S. Lewis, as quoted by Zena Sutherland, "A Matter of Taste," *Saturday Review of Literature*, July 22, 1967, p. 42.

[2] Children's Book Council, 175 Fifth Avenue, New York 10010.

reading conference. Mrs. Priscilla N. Fenn, the center's former director, organized an exhibit in 1964 called the "Expanding Universe of Child-hood." A list of the books from this collection is printed in the catalogue. It includes topics like "Children's Faces Looking Up: picture stories," "No Child Stands Alone: fiction," "Alone in a Multitude: biography," "This Expanding Universe: science." The complete list suggests 138 books which would be a joy to read as well as a foundation for an excellent library serving all ages.

Having "crammed" a course in children's literature, the teacher is ready to share his knowledge with the class. My daily communion takes the form of a half-hour session in the afternoon, when I read aloud books which I have previewed and particularly enjoyed. It seems essential to know the book before involving the children, and to know the children. Some books will not reach a class full of complacent children. Some children will not tolerate rereadings: everything has to be new or they are bored. If this is true, it is time to examine the teacher's attitudes as well. Most children will hear a really good book again, anticipating eagerly and noticing ideas or details in a new light.

EXPECTATIONS

There is always a reason for my book selections. Usually I have in mind at least one of these criteria: a mind-stretching concept, a controversial social issue, a meaningful character, an interesting technique like fantasy, allegory, or humor. The purpose of the book directs the things I ask the class to do at the end. The children are aware that there is some kind of feedback awaiting them, but they are not unduly concerned. They become engrossed in the special book, which they know is not just a time killer.

Literature time is relaxed for all. It is a chance for the children to unwind, to doodle or knit as they listen. Often they sit on the grass in the shade of an old sycamore tree. Since I have a soft voice, I ask the children not to talk during my reading. It is up to each teacher and his class to set standards that are most comfortable for them. (My class discovered that the combination of literature followed by physical education was perfect. The park across the street became Friday's setting for quiet moments and Capture the Flag.) The whole practice grows intimate, even sacred. The children do not want to miss "lit." They do not want substitutes to read to them. They are fierce and dedicated.

I try to vary the length, style and content of my selections, matching the book to the season and the mood of the class. Certain books are particularly good for the beginning of the year, others for presummer reading. The most difficult books, allegories and the like, I read in January through April. Here are three sequences:

1. *The Wheel on the School*—Meindert de Jong
   The Light in the Forest—Conrad Richter
   Winnie the Pooh—A. A. Milne
   North to Freedom—Anne Holm, translated from Danish
   Harriet the Spy—Louise Fitzhugh
   That Quail, Robert—Margaret Stanger
   Island of the Blue Dolphins—Scott O'Dell

2. *Phantom Tollbooth*—Norman Juster and Jules Feiffer
   The Big Wave—Pearl Buck; *Call It Courage*—Armstrong Sperry
   The Village that Slept—Monique Peyrouton de Ladebat, translated from French
   Charlie and the Chocolate Factory—Roald Dahl
   Wrinkle in Time—Madeleine L'Engle
   Dorp Dead—Julia Cunningham
   The Cricket in Times Square—G. Selden
   My Side of the Mountain—Jean George

3. *Bob Fulton's Amazing Soda-Pop Stretcher*—Jerome Beatty, Jr.
   The Legend of Sleepy Hollow—Washington Irving
   The Witch of Blackbird Pond—Elizabeth Speare
   The Rescuers—Margery Sharp
   The Loner—Esther Weik
   It's Like This, Cat—Emily Neville
   Rascal—Sterling North
   Chitty, Chitty, Bang-Bang—Ian Fleming

FEEDBACK: DISCUSSIONS

Given the opportunity, children can make significant responses early in the year. To document their ability, I saved some notes from one discussion. It focuses on a comparison of two books, both written by outstanding craftsmen. The similarities are remarkable, and the differences marked. The underlying problem is really one of semantics: the meaning of the words "compare" and "contrast," two collegiate pitfalls. Like all of my examples, the notes should be read for format and concepts, rather than for any specific knowledge of the books themselves.

Notes on Class Discussion of *THE BIG WAVE* and *CALL IT COURAGE*

(1) <u>Compare</u> Jiya and Mafatu and their problems:

The Big Wave by Pearl Buck	*Call It Courage* by Armstrong Sperry
Jiya: Fisherman's son, family killed by the Big Wave.	Mafatu—"Stout Heart": Chieftain's son. Mother killed by sea goddess.
As a boy: Life with no family. Choice between Kino and Old Man.	As a boy: Life of cowardly boy. Woman's work (making nets, cooking, carving) which helps him later.
As a man: Life with fear. Marriage to Kino's sister. They move back to the beach and build house with window facing the sea, unlike the other fisherman. Life is stronger than death.	As a boy whose manhood has to be proven, Mafatu does the following: a. runs away to island of sacrifice; b. steps over sacred boundaries to show no fear of foreign gods; c. kills wild boar, shark, octopus with knife he has carved; d. builds canoe and returns home; e. conquers fear of sea by retrieving knife underwater and traveling on big waves.

(2) Which character is more sympathetic? Whom do we care for most?
Disagreement, depending on individual reader.

We know less about Jiya's past.	We know more about Mafatu, his personality and past.
His battle is a private one, which he has to win himself.	His battle is a public one, where he has to prove his courage to everyone, as well as himself.

(3) <u>Contrast</u> writing styles in the two stories.

Emphasis on description.	Emphasis on Mafatu and thoughts.
Short sentences, no extra words (no articles in Japanese).	Heavier, more romantic tongue, rich in folklore (more Polynesian).
Conversation between two boys which stresses friendship.	Little conversation—really monologue. No one to talk to except dog.

6. Reading Aloud to Children

ART WORK

Besides discussion, there are other follow-ups which require no writing. Art work, particularly murals, is favored. Depending on the book, there are many possibilities. After finishing *Bob Fulton's Amazing Soda-Pop Stretcher*, a humorous book about a boy who is not to be confused with the man of steamboat fame, the class drew inventions. Their concoctions were fantastic, almost eclipsing those by Rube Goldberg. The draftsmanship and humor in work done by some of the talented older boys recalled graphics by Paul Klee.

Once the class had a Pooh party, inspired by *The Pooh Project Book*.[3] The children played *Pin the Tail on Eeyore* and charades, using quotations from A. A. Milne. (Charades is an art, which is fun to cultivate in the classroom on rainy days for physical education or occasionally during regular class time as a break from routine. If rationalization is needed, charades certainly is a form of communication.) The children munched on *honey* graham crackers and other goodies to tunes sung by Maurice Evans.

WRITTEN WORK

There are also interesting written assignments. The class pursued some of the word games in *The Phantom Tollbooth*. They broke the Hobbit code after reading the first of Tolkien. After *Harriet the Spy*, they kept journals. (Several girls started on their own during the reading. Unlike Harriet, they did not get into trouble.) This book tied in perfectly with one of my practices: each year the children keep a daily record of their thoughts and activities. Sometimes it is in the form of a standard diary, other times it is a poetry journal. In composition books, they write daily entries for a week—about a page a day. An extended period of time is too tiring. (Only the children who forget or write poorly have another week.) Generally, in one week reticent writing is pried open, yet not loosened enough to reveal too much about family affairs. I tell the children that the journals are confidential and nothing will be shown or published without permission. They can write public or private thoughts. The main thing is to get them writing.

There are ordinary writing tasks, too. If the reading relates to social studies, the children take notes. I have given tests, mainly identification of

[3] Another delightful book for Milne fiends like me is *The Pooh Perplex* by Frederick Crewes.

characters or setting. Usually I revert to this type of feedback when the children have been inattentive or I am in a slightly vindictive mood. Like a spanking, a test helps the adult to purge his system and the children soon get over it. It is probably cathartic as long as it is infrequent.

SUGGESTIONS FROM OTHER TEACHERS

Sendak, Maurice, *Where the Wild Things Are*. The text, especially the illustrations, will start the readers thinking about their own nightmares. The children can sit quietly or put their heads down, jotting down ideas before joining the land of the wakeful to write prose or poetry.

White, E. B., *Charlotte's Web*. A delightful book to use at the beginning of the school year to coincide with the autumn just before the Fair (the Fair in the story, that is). "Make up other words that Charlotte could have woven into her web."

Kipling, Rudyard, *Just So Stories*. (The Doubleday edition illustrated by Nicholas is good and reasonably priced.) Before sending the children off to write their own "how" stories, discuss some of the characteristic techniques. This project is particularly good for independent writers who concoct and illustrate many stories.

Ness, Evaline, *Sam, Bangs, and Moonshine*. Read the book just up to the point where Father enters. Ask each child to complete the story from that point on. After all the endings are finished, collected, and perhaps discussed, share the ending as the author wrote it.

chapter seven

DEVELOPING A SENSE
OF FORM

THE FIRST STAGE: READING ALOUD

Reading aloud is one of the best ways to project patterns, social and intellectual, that children can emulate. Using the common experience of a particular book, class members can share their ideas in discussion. They can interact and talk about concepts that might be difficult to put down on paper, like the elements of story structure.

Here are the notes from such a discussion. The children talked about the book after they had recalled in paint the story line and/or their favorite characters. Surrounded by a ring of huge, bright tempera murals as reminders, the children shared their ideas. Again, it is this thinking process rather than details from the book that I wish to highlight.

Climax

1. Problem. Exciting high point in PLOT (story, plan)
2. On the verge of answer—good or bad solution (often more than one, as in *The Wheel on the School*)[1]

Examples

  I. Finding the wheel
     Jella stealing one
     Tinman
     Barn with Eelka
     Wheel in the canal
     Twins with Janus
     Lina and Douwa
     Two Tots in Tower

  II. Getting a wheel on the school in the storm
  III. Getting storks to Shore—Pier on sandbar

Meaning of Book

1. "Sometimes when we wonder, we can make things begin to happen."
2. When you get to know them better, people are different than you thought. ("Nicer" in some cases like Eelka, Janus, Grandmother Sibble III, Everett, Farmer, Douwa.)

When children have heard, let alone participated in several discussions like this one, it is time to move on to even more independent thinking and writing. (The discussions then become valuable as a pool for all the written ideas.)

THE SECOND STAGE: FOLLOWING A MODEL

The second phase is one of quasi independence. The children can write fairly well, following a model before them. They are eager yet unsure of themselves. Their grasp of a particular prose form is tenuous. Two methods are excellent for practicing the concept of plot, as well as for quick diagnoses of writing style and unity. As briefly as possible, they are:

1. Like an old-fashioned "pot-boiler," the teacher goes around a circle and collects a sentence in sequence from each child. The story must finish

---

[1] Meindert de Jong, *The Wheel on the School.*

with the last child. Overnight the teacher transcribes his notes and makes a double-spaced ditto of the story, which he hands out the next day. The children individually edit the story, considering: (a) *Plot*—Are there any inconsistencies or sudden jumps in the story? If you find any, try to fix them. (b) *Style*—Are there any details that would enrich the story, or any words that should be left out? Within the limits of the page, add or subtract them. (The children need not waste time by recopying the story, unless absolutely necessary. To avoid calamity, it is a good idea to have them use pencil.)

2. Each child submits three scraps of paper. On one piece he has written a place (setting); on each of the other two, a person (character) that is real or fictitious. The teacher places the slips in three separate containers. Each child draws a slip from each container. Armed with two characters and a setting, he goes in search of a story. The combinations are usually delightful and absurd: Francis Scott Key steals fame and fortune from Bugs Bunny in Japan, Mr. Magoo and Shirley Temple go to Princeton University, Liz Taylor on Mars meets her sixth husband, Dr. Kildare.

THE THIRD STAGE: EXPLORING OWN IDEAS

The writing in this stage is independent and original. If models are suggested, they are enjoyed, considered, and then usually reinterpreted or abandoned. The children rely far more on their own resources and experiences. (Sometimes the teacher does not recognize this as the farthest point of development. He instead penalizes a creative child for being "obstinate" or "tangential.")

The teacher should continue seeking new and exciting ways to exercise various forms of prose. As always, books provide the best ideas for classroom use. After reading *Wrinkle in Time*,[2] I realized that science fiction could be fascinating. Well-written, it is just an extension of fantasy. Needing a model situation for the short story, I decided to exploit the fact that most children in this scientific age adore "the step beyond." They were given two weeks for a short-story assignment.

Mythology can be modernized, too. Or examples can be appreciated from different cultures, rather than from the usual and lovely Greco-Roman civilization. A colleague, who developed a useful unit on classical mythology,[3] suggests a project of "allusion collecting" from literature, art,

[2] Madeleine L'Engle, *Wrinkle in Time*.

[3] Gay Collins, *Mythology* (unpublished; June 1967).

and advertising. This aspect might be an interesting follow-up to the hogwash experience (Television–Chapter II above). The children could become familiar with myths by gathering references from daily life: the messenger from "Flowers by Wire," who is really the messenger of the gods; Atlas Company, movers; Pegasus, the trademark of a well-known oil company; Mercury, an automobile; Ajax, a cleanser. The more sophisticated might realize that Pygmalion and Galatea inspired Shaw's play *Pygmalion* and later the musical adaptation, *My Fair Lady*; Daphnis and Chloe furnished the theme for a suite by Ravel; Shakespeare's *Romeo and Juliet* comes from the story of Pyramus and Thisbe from late Greek legend; Orpheus and Eurydice inspired the modern film, *Black Orpheus.* A few art books in the classroom would provide examples from the Renaissance or seventeenth century that are neoclassical. Rubens and Bernini are typical.

The results were handsome, even though basically the assignment was "just to write a story." The added attraction of science fiction made all the difference.

By the same token, the fable became intriguing when the element of the modern (rather than that of the future) was introduced. James Thurber's *Fables for Our Time* was a wonderful springboard for fractured fables with crooked morals. I certainly do not mean to advocate anarchy–by no means "Down with Aesop and LaFontaine!" On the contrary, I expect a happy familiarity with the old masters, so that older children can build on top of that foundation.

7. Developing a Sense of Form   79

chapter eight

DEVELOPING CRITICAL JUDGMENT

A WORD TO THE WISE

The first two processes, story-hearing and story-making, which develop an aural and a written sense of form, establish the third dimension of literature: critical judgment. The gradual build-up of a fund of criteria from classroom discussions and written work really pays dividends. It is a common fallacy that anyone, especially a talented substitute or supporting teacher, can walk into a classroom and *teach* language. (Perhaps I am possessive and prejudiced by the things that "my" children have written for other adults.)

Written work, particularly of the creative and critical type, is very intimate. Sharing innermost thoughts requires basic trust. It is difficult for

LITERATURE CLASS: THINGS TO LOOK FOR IN YOUR READING

A. Style of the book

   1. What kinds of words does the author use? Descriptive, poetic, factual?

   2. Does he use much dialect or slang? Why?

   3. Does the author include conversation or a great deal of description?

   4. Are the paragraphs and sentences long or short? What effect does this create?

   5. What effect does the author's style have on making the books interesting, easy to read or memorable?

B. Format of the book

   1. Binding. Cloth or paper cover? Sturdy? Of good quality?

   2. Paper. Too shiny? Too thin? Too yellow?

   3. Type face. Fussy? Uneven? Too small? Easy to read?

   4. Spacing. Attractive? Crowded?

   5. Illustrations. Appropriate to text? Realistic? Imaginative? Colorful?

   6. End papers, margin designs. Attractive, dull?

C. Plot of book

   1. Does the plot unfold gradually or suddenly?

   2. Is there a surprise ending? If so, what was your reaction to it?

   3. Does the book have much suspense, or is it more a study of character or the solving of a problem?

   4. Is there a climax? When does it occur?

   5. Is the ending satisfying or disturbing? Why?

D. Characters in the book

   1. Who is the main character? Do you like or dislike him or her? Why?

   2. Do the personalities of the characters change during the story? What causes these changes? What were the effects of these changes?

   3. Would you want to be like or to change places with any of the characters in the book? Why?

LITERATURE CLASS: THINGS TO LOOK FOR IN YOUR READING

Standards for evaluating a book

a. Soundness of story structure

Importance of theme

Interest of plot, determined by

The flow of action in the story

The logic of the sequence of events

The absence of distracting detail or action

Completeness of story, including

An introduction answering who, what, when, where, why

Body or content which develops the central problem or conflict

A climax which is logically reached

A conclusion which is satisfying, uncontrived

b. Effectiveness of style

Vividness of word pictures

Effectiveness of setting and mood

Suitability of style for theme and plot

c. Effectiveness of characterization

Clarity, vividness, distinctiveness, and plausibility of characterization

Degree of empathy, sympathy or antagonism aroused in the reader

Memorability or inspirational value of characters

d. Satisfaction given the reader

Insight the reader gains in human problems, including possibly his own

Pleasure the reader receives

Knowledge the reader gains

Emotional involvement the reader feels

a child or an adult to expose his innate self in front of a stranger. For that reason I am opposed to such departmentalization as special literature groups pasted together from various classrooms in the name of enrichment. The situation is too artificial. For the best results, each teacher should handle his own language program. He should enrich himself, so that he has more to offer.

Some teachers bombard their classes with reams of guide sheets. Consequently, the children's writing is prefabricated. All the questions and details, even the choice of adjectives, are listed. No one goes beyond the guide to dig for his own theories. He would be foolish to waste time and energy, when the satisfactory requirements are spelled out. Who works hard, when the minimum is at hand?

To the observer who has not seen the dittoed mold, the product is glib, perhaps impressive. The result is dishonest, catering to tight adult expectations. I include here two examples of such guide sheets to give the reader an example of a trap which sometimes ensnares overzealous teachers. The checklist does not totally lack "redeeming social value," because it is helpful as background for the teacher. It would be far better, however, to read a real critic or to take a course in literature for adults. (After all, the concepts are the same for children.)

The guide sheets are sometimes useful for adaptation. I have altered and prescribed them in small doses. I much prefer giving the children a specific assignment which focuses on a single concept. They become familiar with the idea by toying with it alone. The teacher can afford to let the task be open-ended when there is a central and experimental theme, rather than a perplexing lot of shallow alternatives.

CONSTRUCTIVE ASSIGNMENTS

If they relax, children can be great builders. Some of their best critical writings come from problems in which they have to construct a type or a picture of the times. I offer three examples of assignments which evoke thoughtful responses from independent young critics. The first was, as its heading indicates, a preparation for a library trip. The other two were given later, in different years, with the idea of using literature as a primary source in social studies. (Pages 84 and 85.)

The ensuing responses of two boys to the last of these assignments are not typical. Their natural writing styles and interesting ideas, documented by specific facts and quotations, are already close to the epitome that

PREPARATION: Library trip on May 18th

1. Choose a Newbery book you haven't read before.

2. Read it carefully, then decide what is special about the book.
   (You might find it helpful to consider the old standbys of
   plot, character, style.)

Assignment due two weeks from today:

Write two pages on the following question:

''What are some of the reasons for the selection of the Newbery
Award?'' (In other words, can you say anything about Newbery
books in general? Remember, you have heard several in class this
year--Wrinkle in Time, Call It Courage, Twenty-one Balloons. Use
these class readings, as well as any ideas or comparisons from
other winners you have enjoyed. You don't need to do any research
at the library!)

Revolutionary Verse from a Philadelphia Newspaper

''It may be read in three different ways--1st. Let the whole be read
in the order in which it is written; 2d. Then the lines downward on the
left of each comma in every line; and 3d. In the same manner on the right
of each comma.''

Hark! Hark the trumpet sounds, the din of war's alarms,

O'er seas and solid grounds, doth call us all to arms;

Who for King George doth stand, their honors soon shall shine;

Their ruin is at hand, who with the Congress join.

The acts of Parliament, in them I much delight,

I hate their cursed intent, who for the Congress fight,

The Tories of the day, they are my daily toast,

They soon will sneak away, who Independence boast;

Who non-resistance hold, they have my hand and heart.

May they for slaves be sold, who act a Whiggish part;

On Mansfield, North and Bute, may daily blessings pour,

Confusion and dispute, on Congress evermore;

To North and British Lords, may honors still be done,

I wish a block or cord, to General Washington.

```
                    LIVING IN THE LAST CENTURY

Procedure:

(1) Choose one book or story by one of these writers (Alcott, Cooper,
    Harte, Hawthorne, Irving, Twain, Wilder or other ''approved''
    writers.)

(2) Read it carefully and begin to think about these issues:

    a. Details of life at that time

        For example, do they have things we do not use today; Do
        they do things we would not?

    b. Would the characters fit into ''modern Western life?''

(3) Decide:

    a. How true does the whole story seem to you?  Do you have any
       evidence?

    b. Does it seem to tie in with the author's experience?
```

many of us seek. Their essays do show the upper range of expression and contact with good works of American literature, opportunities which might not be open to them in traditional elementary-school tasks.

Bret Harte – "Tennessee's Partner"

People in those days thought death wasn't that bad. When Tennessee died (got hanged), the funeral was very informal and there wasn't much sorrow. There was even a little humor from some of the men! (Harte says that a person who came to Sandy Bar was judged partly by his humor. Then Harte talks about humor on and off for the rest of the story.) The cemeteries were too expensive, so people buried their friends or family next to their houses.

Sandy Bar was a dirty place. Like most bars in that day, it was the social center of town. The men would rather hang around than work, so most of them were poor. They didn't care.

[A paragraph has been omitted here.]

8. Developing Critical Judgment   85

It wasn't bad, compared to today, to have a fight. Men at the bar would settle arguments by fists instead of words. Before Tennessee was hanged, the men made a jury from people who frequented Sandy Bar. This probably made the trial unfair.

Children weren't half as free as they are today. In school they were whipped if they were late or did something bad. In their classes they did their work out loud! The school had one classroom, but it was big. The different grades sat in different parts of the room.

[Bill B., age 11]

Bret Harte—"The Luck of Roaring Camp"

In a camp in the west (Harte never tells what state it's in, but my guess is California) some men are having an argument. There is an Indian Woman about to have a baby. A woman in camp is enough, but a baby is sensational. They even make bets on the baby's sex. After it is born, the woman dies. Then the men adopt him, and even christen him. This is highly unusual for rough, tough miners. They name him "The Luck" and protect him in every way.

One day they get a warning of a flood. Stumpy, the leader, said that "The Luck" would protect him. (These men are quite superstitious, a trait of many miners.) The next night, the flood comes. Stumpy is drowned, and another man, Kentuck, is dying when they find him. He has "Luck" who is dead. Kentuck says, "Tell the boys I've got the luck with me now." He feels secure as he dies.

[Cameron M., age 11]

READING AND COMPREHENSION

At this point, it is important to note that these assignments are not required for all reading. I limit them to the shared class experiences of literature or occasional independent projects, so that the children enjoy and broaden their understanding of books. By no means do I recommend constant follow-up for reading programs, selective or otherwise. Too much is made of reading and comprehension, in terms of direct feedback like standard book reports, sentence completions, and tests. Educators want concrete proof that the reader has understood what he has seen. Their guidelines are often dry and stereotyped, more threatening than stimulating.

Children need to know that reading is basically a private activity. After all, grownups are allowed to read and enjoy books by themselves, internalizing or storing their reactions without any outside demands. If the books are meaningful, they become part of the reader at some time or another. Adults do not need to justify their selection or comprehension of books all the time.

Most systems that teachers adopt to justify their reading programs are artificial and stultifying. They expect too much from the excellent students, who are penalized for their avid reading, and from the poor students, who are further alienated. For instance, "Fifty ways of reporting a book," using an elaborate chart with stars to keep track of plays, pantomimes, artwork, or the like, is a fatuous approach to reading. Asking the child to read aloud daily or weekly, while the teacher takes elaborate notes, is usually not worth the investment of time, except for the personal contact with the students.

There is no easy answer to this dilemma. The teacher must frequently ask himself: "Is my approach honest? Do I really encourage reading?" "Do I have real information, not busywork, that I can share with the parents?" Over the years only one of my systems has satisfied these criteria and the test of time . . . for me! Each child keeps a simple record of his reading throughout the year. When he finishes a book, he enters the author, title, and date of completion on one line on a filecard. He rates the book "+" (good), "–" (poor) or "0" (indifferent). All of the filecards are stored in a filebox, centrally located so that the children can refer to them for recommended books, as well as for additions to their cards. This method is quite painless, yet informative. The teacher and parents can get a good idea of a child's reading profile—the type of books and frequency. So can the students!

If the writing program is strong, somewhat as described, reading does not need to be a separate subject with lots of ritual. Mainly, the children need a quiet period and a comfortable place to read. I think the best booster to promote reading would be for the teacher to sprawl out and read a good book by himself—in the class as well as at home. On this relaxed note, I end Part II. Part III on poetry picks up where this section on literature leaves off, with the use of great books.

part three

POETRY

chapter nine

APPROACH

To write good poetry, children must hear and see great poetry. Too often teachers read trite verse to their children, half apologetically: "Poetry is painful, so I will give you some easy rhymes to introduce you to this unnatural realm." Some adults simply lack any feeling for poetry and disguise their ignorance by teaching dry techniques.[1] If these teachers feel uncomfortable or threatened and keep a closed mind, it would be better for them to skip the whole notion of poetry rather than contaminate the classroom with unlovely ideas.

For the thinking person, there is no need to have a big hang-up about poetry. All of the routes discussed in the section on prose lead to poetic statements: viewpoint, open-ended questions, serendipity, word games,

---

[1] One of my English teachers in high school did the unforgiveable act: by assigning us various poems to read and asking us to reduce their meanings to one prose sentence, he nearly turned the whole class against poetry. It took all the effort and charms of another English teacher in my senior year to right this wrong.

and literature. If the children have been successful using prose forms, their enjoyment will spread to poetry. An adventurous program in prose sets the pace for the class. The children relax, experiment, and trust. They reveal their inner thoughts.

I love poetry, but I don't make a big fuss over it in the initial stage. Before anything is mentioned at all about poetry, I like to read to the children from some of my favorite poets. If possible, the children have copies of the poems in front of them. They follow along as I read. After listening, they put away the dittoes for safekeeping; thus ends the first poetry session.

A few days later, the class reads the poems again. It is important for children to see and hear the poems more than once, for sheer pleasure as well as for added understanding. Extra encounters should be varied so that the class will not become "conditioned" or bored.

The children begin to share some of their reactions—words they savored, meanings and double meanings. Frost's titles—like "Once by the Pacific," "The Runaway," "Canis Major"—are excellent examples of literary irony. This session gets lively. (A teacher should not worry about occasional lapses in the discussion and try to fill in the gaps with adult insights, like an overanxious host. A class is only as comfortable as its teacher. It takes a while for thought and controversy to stir. Someone will take the initiative.)

By looking at several poems by one writer, the class can begin to speculate "Where is he from?" "What kind of a man is (was) he?" Robert Frost and Carl Sandburg are exciting subjects. The children, encouraged by the teacher, begin to take risks. They grow presumptuous and delightful, as they try to decide "What is poetry to these two gentlemen?" They formulate definitions. At the end of the discussion, or the beginning of the next, I confront them with several definitions by the poets; for example, "Poetry is what you see between the opening and closing of the door" (Carl Sandburg). Robert Frost used to tell the students in his college classes to search for the common in experience and to make it uncommon in expression. If possible I use several definitions by the same poet at different times. The research is worthwhile, because the children realize that poetry, or art in general, does not have a single, stationary meaning even for one man.

The children discover that the essence of poetry is very personal. It is this quality, rather than form, which should be stressed in the teaching and writing of poetry. In this case, form does follow function (or meaning).

The children feel free to search through their own experiences, sorting out the good, the *true*, and maybe the beautiful.

The reader may well ask, "What relevance does this have for children of primary age?" After spending a summer in a workshop for creative experiences in early childhood, I am convinced that there is no use in teaching little ones poetry. The best that one can do is prepare them for poetry with intriguing prose or a wide range of read-aloud poems. Most of the available anthologies for younger children are poor, perhaps because the category is artificial.

Teachers are either "projecting" or elevating what they see, if they imagine poems have been produced in their kindergartens. (I have also seen teachers doctor prose into *quasi haiku*. At times, I shudder at the basic misdirection of education, perpetrated by schoolmarms.) The children write naive and charming ideas which the adult reinterprets and enjoys. The writings are beautiful in the eyes of the beholder, which is wonderful, but they are not poems. Young children think in terms of narrative and sing-song patterns. Their expression has not yet risen to the uncommon. Depending on the children, of course, the turning point seems to be around nine or ten years old. I must, however, acknowledge another opinion: Flora Arnstein[2] waxes ecstatic about the poetry of little people.

[2] *Children Write Poetry: A Creative Approach.*

chapter ten

POETS

The teacher does some of the work, but Robert Frost and Carl Sandburg do more and better. They set a mood of simplicity and honesty which is essential for writing. They also use a precious ingredient, humor, which disarms reluctant children who have been raised on tedious verse. All kinds of misconceptions are dispelled. Poets can be funny. They can be bewildered, like Carl Sandburg in "Arithmetic." They can be interested in baseball or in movie stars. ("The Chillicothe Players" and "Lines Written for Gene Kelly to Dance to" are also written by the Prairie Poet. The latter poem really captures the rhythm of casual tappings and masculine steps which made the dancer famous. It is found in *Windsong*,[1] an excellent

[1] Carl Sandburg, *Wind Song*, New York, Harcourt, Brace, 1953.

collection of his poems which appeal to young readers as well as adults.) Poets can hold other jobs: witness respectable middle-aged, middle-class men in insurance and medicine like Wallace Stevens and William Carlos Williams. In short, poets can be human.

Since poets are people, children will respond to them differently—on an individual basis. Rather than accept all poems as sacred, the children will pick favorites. What could be better? Thus, the teacher will have a variety of poets in the class. It is not hard to discern which poet this girl prefers:

Icicles

If you have ever lived in New England during the winter, you must have seen and heard icicles melting. It is a beautiful sound, like the tinkling of silver bells. Slowly at first, they melt faster and faster. Finally they disappear.

>Plurp, splut,
>Dripping water,
>Slowly melting icicles,
>Royal scepters from another land
>Disappearing from ours.
>
>Slowly at first,
>Telling of golden ponds,
>Of silver swans,
>Of elfin yawns.
>
>Faster, faster,
>Singing of gurgling streams,
>Of sapphire dreams,
>Of golden beams
>Of a silver sun.
>
>Rushing faster,
>Disappearing
>Like cloudy diamonds,
>Disappearing
>They go.

[Sara M., age 11]

This poem has beautiful phrasing up to the last stanza. The last lines tend to weaken the whole, a very tempting situation for an editor. However, I have left them in because the poem would lose its sense of unity and purpose. Sometimes a child writes verse with awkward rhythms and perhaps one lovely line, where poetry begins. The awkward rhythm will smooth out as the child grows more assured. Red pencils and blue pencils should be used to praise rather than criticize, underscoring positive points. Otherwise, children are not really encouraged to seek or recognize the uncommon in expression.

Once the children understand the essence of poetry, the teacher can feel free to experiment with form. He does not need to invent new ideas—that is for the poet to do. All the teacher needs to do is read.

Coralie Howard suggests the use of motion in form in *The First Book of Verse*, an outstanding little anthology: "William Carlos Williams was not only a poet, but also a doctor, trained in careful observation. Do you see what the cat is doing in this poem? Do the short lines suggest the cat's motions?

> As the cat
> climbed over
> the top of
>
> the jamcloset
> first the right
> forefoot
>
> carefully
> then the hind stepped down
>
> into the pit of
> the empty
> flowerpot."[2]

I copied this idea and the poem on a ditto, setting the type to the extreme left and leaving space on the right for drawing the action. Some children staged the motions of the cat like an animated cartoon. Their draftsmanship was masterful. They really got the feel of the suspended action and understood the suspense of stepping into the unknown.

Inspired, I also added an idea of my own. I attached another page to the ditto with a poem by E. E. Cummings. This poet and painter appeals to children, who are amazed by his style. Unfortunately most of his work is too controversial for childish eyes and ears. The following is one of his "acceptable" poems:

---

[2] William Carlos Williams, *Collected Earlier Poems.* Copyright 1938 by William Carlos Williams. Reprinted by permission of New Directions Publishing Corporation.

in Just-
spring   when the world is mud-
luscious the little
lame balloonman

whistles   far   and wee

and eddieandbill come
running from marbles and
piracies and it's
spring

when the world is puddle-wonderful

the queer
old balloonman whistles
far   and   wee
and bettyandisbel come dancing

from hop-scotch and jump-rope and

it's
spring
and
        the

                goat-footed

balloonMan   whistles
far
and
wee³

---

³ Copyright, 1923, 1951 by E. E. Cummings. Reprinted from his volume, *Poems 1923-1954* by permission of Harcourt, Brace & World, Inc.

At the end of the sheet, there was this comment: "Now it's your turn to play with motion and the reader's sense of timing. Try to pick a subject that lends itself to action."

Before the children turned loose, they wondered about the spacings and lack of capital letters. They noticed "far and wee" immediately, explaining the spacing as distance. Some of the more "subtle" children realized that "eddieandbill" and "bettyandisbel" were grouped together for at least two reasons: (1) they are good, *close* friends, (2) the pairs are moving fast, running and dancing. Such observations prepared the class for meaningful departures from tradition. The unspoken lesson was that poetic license is not arbitrary or irresponsible.

The results from this kind of thinking and playing are exciting. It is going to be difficult to limit the examples to the following, because the whole class was successful.

The Reader

The eyes of a busy reader
follow along line
after line.
The page turns
And
again the eyes
of the busy reader
go hurriedly along the page
and
the eyes of a busy reader
finish a chapter.
The book snaps shut.

[Sue P., age 9]

A cat's
tongue,
Tiny slurps.

In
and
Out

Drinking
milk.

Pink roughness
back and
forth.

[Margot M., age 11]

Part Three: POETRY

The Icecreamman

it is summer
    here comes the icecreamman
and here comes billylarrybettydavidhugh—
markdenispeterjohnrobert   and little gregg!

                                                      [Denis F., age 10]

         Inchworm

         The small tiny inchworm
         moves slowly,
         first the back
         curls up
         then the front
         straightens out.

         Up the bark
         inch by inch.

         Carefully
         exploring a hole
         in the tree.

              [Diane S., age 10]

Some of the poems may seem slightly derivative. However, each child-poet could justify his choice of subject and form. Perhaps *The Icecreamman* is particularly suspect. At first glance, only the season and the vendor have been changed from the poem by E. E. Cummings. On closer inspection, the reader can see that the focus shifts from close friends in the famous poem to the eager ice-cream eaters and "little Gregg," who can't quite keep up with the crowd. In this instance, a boy picked up an idea from a well-known poet and pursued it further, at least in terms of his own experience. (Denis F. names all of his buddies, including himself, like a renaissance patron in an altarpiece!) A teacher, hasty to judge, might overlook this poem or attribute it to "copying." A few moments of careful reading of each child's work is never wasted. They might save months of rebuilding a shattered ego.

I make it a policy never to accuse anyone for lack of originality, because a child may not yet trust himself or the teacher. Occasionally, a specific question which isn't threatening can direct him away from vague generalities, yet leave him with a feeling that he is self-sufficient.

As an alternative to motion poems, shape poems are also fun. The two look enough alike to confuse some children, so it may be better not to give both to the same class; they can be alternated in successive years. Basically, shape poems are poems which have been styled into the outline of the subject. Dylan Thomas experimented with this genre—lesser poets, too.

SURPRISE!

Your assignment is <u>not</u> to make a <u>haiku.</u> Instead look at this poem by an American named Wallace Stevens, then choose a topic that you can look at from thirteen ways and write some short Japanese-like poems.

<u>Thirteen Ways of Looking at a Blackbird</u>

(Here are only four)

I.

Among twenty snowy mountains

The only moving thing

Was the eye of the blackbird.

II.

I was of three minds

Like a tree

In which there are three blackbirds.

X.

The river is moving.

The blackbird must be flying.

XIII.

It was evening all afternoon.

It was snowing

And it was going to snow.

The blackbird sat

In the cedar limbs.

For his delightful anthology, *The Birds and the Beasts Were There*, William Cole found the "Nightsong of the Fish." Christian Morgenstern, its playful poet, arranged ‒'s and ◡'s (the versificationist's longs and shorts!) for the body and scales. Lewis Carroll experimented with a mouse's tail. Other people have tried Christmas trees, lollipops, flowers—the possibilities are endless. It is important to stress that the poem should be written first and then molded into an appropriate form. Otherwise the children could get carried away with artwork rather than writing.

One of my favorite assignments is based on a poem by Wallace Stevens, as well as an understanding of Japanese *tanka* and *haiku*[4]—their mood and form. Most of the children were very familiar with *haiku* and needed only a brief review. After a quick discussion, I handed them the "Surprise" ditto.

The children grew aware of the poet's intent, using very mechanical methods at first. They counted the number of syllables in each line and discovered that the pattern of the first "way" was 8-6-7; of the second, 5-3-7; of the tenth, 6-7; of the thirteenth, 8-4-7-4-5. The American poet did not stick to the rigid Japanese forms.

After tallying the four stanzas, the children examined each section more carefully. They visualized the contrasts of color or lack of color, black on white and white on black—particularly strong in the first and last stanzas. They saw the motion of the blinking eye against the background of still mountains, the division of a mind from indecision, and the shifts of viewpoint. The class decided that Wallace Stevens had definitely captured the mood of Japanese poetry.

By the end of the week, Mr. Stevens had company. The children produced some of the finest writing I have ever seen, using their new knowledge and sensitivity. The following examples are untouched by adult hands. They are solely from the minds of ten- and eleven-year-olds who looked and thought and wrote.

Thirteen Ways of Looking at the Moon

The moon is a hole
cut in the black paper of sky.

The earth has a little friend
tagging along through space.

[Philip F.]

---

[4] See Chapter Twelve for further treatment.

Ten Ways of Looking at an Umbrella

Wind blowing umbrellas away
Millions of colors swirling around
Wet rainbows.

An umbrella chases the wind
Which is faster?

Dignified gentlemen
go down the street
with their walking umbrellas.

[Jill Z.]

Four Ways of Looking at Seeds

Twenty-seven seeds
my hamster can hold
in her pouches.

I put some seeds
in a hole,
nothing happened.

It's the beginning
of all life we know,
the seed.

We eat seeds,
walnuts, Brazil nuts,
cashew, peanuts and pecans.

[Rod J.]

Thirteen Ways of Looking at a Spider

I.

The spider's web swings,
He holds on with all his strength
Until the wind stops.

VI.

Walking home from school,
I see a spider crawling
Into a small hole.

X.

Clips, rulers, pencils,
A schoolroom with a spider
Snooping in the desks.

XIII.

The spider's running
Away from a big flashlight.
Darkness swallows him.

[Cameron M.]

Part Three: POETRY

I.

I see the sun,
Its glory and splendor,
A circle of light.

II.

I see a glow,
A piercing stare,
A cat's green eye.

III.

Cuckoo! Cuckoo!
The clock moves on,
A circle of time.

V.

Whack, slam,
Homerun,
A baseball.

VII.

Dirty and grimy,
Sweaty from many hands,
A doorknob.

VIII.

Jingle, jangle,
Clinking, clanking,
Silver dollars.

XII.

Killing thousands,
No caution.
A car's wheels.

XIII.

The wheel is turning,
Never ceasing,
The wheel of life.

[Margot M.]

chapter eleven

OTHER VOICES

With lesser poets, the teacher has to do more of the work to get a mood or an idea across to his class. Some anthologies have a dominant theme which is worth pursuing; others merely have a captivating title. With a little bit of effort and discretion, practically everything can be used. Ideas for poetry can be salvaged from almost any reading with second-hand but imaginative results.

The anthologies to which I refer are anthropological as well as beautiful in nature. After listening to *The Sun is a Golden Earring*,[1] some children pretended that they were a "primitive" people explaining the universe. Others used contemporary terms.

The sun is a cat's eye, chasing a rat's tail through the heavens.

[Mike R., age 10]

---

[1] Natalie Belting, *The Sun Is a Golden Earring.*

The sun is a big orange (Sunkist).

[Michael B., age 7]

> The sun is the shield
> Of Ares, the god.
> He hangs it there
> Where no man will trod.
>
> If a man should come
> And take the shield away,
> He could only keep it
> For a year and a day.
>
> For Ares would come
> And take it again,
> Hanging it back
> Where it all began.
>
> [Anne S., age 9]

The moon is a tennis ball that a giant hit into the air.

[Russ W., age 7]

The sun is a ball of yellow yarn. One day a great wind came and blew it away.

[Melinda F., age 9]

The Earth Is on a Fish's Back[2] tells longer stories about the world and the sky, which lend themselves to inventions in prose. Because of its unusual sources, the book would be an excellent basis for comparing myths from exotic places with those from the Hellenic region.

Because there are several handsome sources of information and inspiration, the life of an Eskimo stirs children to write. Using the fine collection of poetry and color photographs in *Beyond the High Hills*[3] or the reproductions in *Art of the Eskimo*,[4] children can imagine the daily struggles of the hunting season and the relaxed moments during slack periods.

[2] Natalie Belting, *The Earth Is on a Fish's Back*.

[3] Knud Rasmussen, *Beyond the High Hills*.

[4] Shirley Glubok, *Art of the Eskimo*. Other books in the series deal with art in the ancient world.

There is joy
When I set my teeth
To smile and to laugh
Like others who do.

[Carmen L., age 11]

Nothing can surpass the old but startling realism of a two-reeler, *Nanook*. (Most film libraries have it.) The film is worth two showings with a little space in between.[5] After seeing this movie, the children will write all kinds of observations which may or may not turn into striking poems of simplicity.

William Cole collects poetry for adults and children. The title alone of one anthology, *Beastly Boys and Ghastly Girls*, would be a very good assignment to milk the venom of the sexes. I have not tried that idea in class yet, but I have used another one of his volumes, *The Birds and the Beasts Were There*. This book has poems by well-known writers with humor and imagination, and handsome woodcuts by Helen Siegl. It appeals to children and encourages them to pick unusual subjects, animal or insect, as well as to try new forms.

A plover and a clover:
A clover gives you luck,
A plover is a kind of bird
That lives on sand and muck.

[Adam K., age 11]

Too often teachers throw the children a bone—a vague assignment: "Write a poem on your favorite animal." Neither party has a notion of the possibilities, so the results are forced and trite, definitely unsatisfying. The remedy is to be specific—for instance, by reading *The Book of Practical Cats* by T. S. Eliot. (For the teacher who does not like to read poetry aloud, there is a record performed by the late poet himself.) The children then have the option to write about cats, domestic or wild, or to choose some other subject. In any case, they will have heard some amusing rhymes about a favorite animal by a major poet.

[5] A rare commendation for me. While I am a visually oriented person, I despise all the time-killing hours in school that many schoolchildren spend watching "educational" films or television. In such classrooms, these devices no longer are visual aids but boring crutches, which teachers accept without any previews to lighten their teaching loads.

Part Three: POETRY

There are many beautiful animal stories like *The Bat-Poet* by Randall Jarrell; interesting biographies like *Rascal* by Sterling North and *That Quail, Robert* by Margaret Stanger; haunting studies like *Creatures of Darkness* by Esther and Leonard Baskin, intimate descriptions like *King Solomon's Ring* by Konrad Lorenz, *Rain in the Woods and Other Small Matters* by Glen Rounds, or those by Sally Carrighar.[6] There is no excuse for not piling up a rich reserve of experiences which the children can use in poetry. Poetry is not a "sometime thing."

Three women—Mary O'Neill, Eve Merriam, and Elizabeth Coatsworth—have written books of poetry that are perfect for use in the classroom. In one way or another, I have enjoyed two by Mary O'Neill: *Hailstones and Halibut Bones* and *People I'd Like to Keep*. Teachers have widely used the book and the movie of *Hailstones* for motivating poems on color. (Nina Walter has some splendid ideas like "Adventure in Green" in her book,[7] which brightens the palette.) Girls usually write fantastic and rhapsodic verse, while the boys are realistic.

> Gold
> is the color
> of millionaires
> and old people's cavities.
>
> [Randy F., age 10]

Somehow the contents of her second book do not live up to its intriguing title. I do not read the poems from *People I'd Like to Keep* to the children. Instead I wave the book in front of the class and read the cover to them. Then I ask them to write poems to fill the pages of the book. They choose people who are not in the room—famous, unfamous and infamous.

Washington is one I'd like to keep,
Napoleon before Waterloo.
I'd like to own famous people.
You would, too.

[Robert S., age 9]

I'd like to keep
a plump little girl
an almost perfect girl
a pretty teacher
but most of all,
myself.

[Kathy F., age 11]

[6] See the Bibliography for complete citations.

[7] Nina Walter, *Let Them Write Poetry*.

11. Other Voices

A third book by Mary O'Neill has wonderful possibilities. *Words Words Words* puts grammar in verse, dealing with punctuation and parts of speech in a succinct manner.

Of several good books written by Eve Merriam, my favorite is *There is No Rhyme for Silver*. One of her poems intrigued me sufficiently to be used as an assignment for geography as well as poetry. In "Geography," she names a product for each of thirty-seven states. To complete the poem, however, she invokes the participation of the reader, who must discover thirteen states and their abbreviations.

I saved Elizabeth Coatsworth for the last of these three ladies because she is very special. Her poetry rings true and beautiful. There is nothing at all contrived or cute about her work. She has the instincts of a teacher as well as those of a poet. She chooses subjects for her poems that can be used in the classroom.

I have never forgotten my first introduction to her, an excerpt from "Poem of Praise" in Mauree Applegate's book, *Helping Children To Write*:

> And slow things are beautiful;
> the closing of day,
> the pause of the wave
> that curves downward to spray,
> the ember that crumbles,
> the opening flower,
> and the ox that moves on
> in the quiet of power.[8]

The opening line suggests a topic for a description or a poem, which children can complete. The poem itself is a lovely example of subtle rhyme and effective sounds, techniques which the youngest poets need to know.

The Children Come Running is an unusual book of poetry by Miss Coatsworth, using as illustrations and presumably as inspiration the drawings of children from the UNICEF calendars. Finally finding a good use for my old appointment books, I tore mine apart. I posted ten bright drawings by children from all over the world on a bulletin board in front of the children from a small town in California. The idea sparked. The spaces I had left beneath each of the pictures filled up with poems: some haiku, some rhymes, some free verse. In this way we celebrated United Nations Day in October.

---

[8] Reprinted with permission of The Macmillan Company from "Swift Things Are

Part Three: POETRY

"Settlement"—Ivory Coast [Lamory Dominique, age 15]
Shankar Children's Competition; UNICEF

Calypso

Meeting in the dark
Talking, singing,
Doing a chore
Come back tomorrow
Talk some more.

[Janie C., age 9]

"Huts"—Bulgaria [Ivanka Dimitrova Pancheva, age 8]
Shankar Children's Competition; UNICEF

A bright little village
So gay and merry
As the smoke comes
Out of the chimneys
Looking like cherries.
[Cathy E., age 9]

Part Three: POETRY

"In the Zoo"—Czechoslovakia [Eva Pavlickova, age 8]
Shankar Children's Competition; UNICEF

I will show my strength
and courage to man
some day.
[Melinda F., age 9]

To end this section appropriately, I must share an idea developed by one of the boys in a recent class. He based a poem on an actual quotation from a book called *The Dictionary of Last Words*,[9] a collection of sayings from the deathbeds of notables. It is certainly a variation of the standard procedure where a teacher gives his class a first line.

H. G. Wells—Famous Last Words

H. G. Wells, feeling worse,
sat up to face a bossy nurse
and then he said with fighting might,
"Go away, I'm all right."
As H. G. Wells laid in bed,
his blood ran cold,
his heart stopped dead.
Away she went, this bossy nurse
but so did he—she'd called the hearse.

[Clay J., age 10]

[9] Edward. S. Le Compte, *The Dictionary of Last Words*, New York Philosophical Library, 1955, p. 212.

chapter twelve

FORM

As the reader knows by now, I do not give any premium to form for its own sake. However, two types of forms, though somewhat demanding, are understandable and enjoyable for elementary poets: haiku and limericks.

HAIKU

I need to spend some time discussing haiku, because the form is popular and because it is mistreated. The haiku is deceptively simple. Hence, teachers grab it to enhance their study of Japan or to make their language program more exotic and esoteric. If they have gained their knowledge by hearsay rather than by research, they seldom understand the form and its essence. The results are diluted images with forced phrases which are far from the intent of classical haiku.

113

The best source of information on the development and subtleties of haiku is a brief booklet published by the Japan Society.[1] The concepts are clear: however, the examples are drab in comparison with other sources. I will try to combine the best of both worlds here.

There are several rules to bear in mind, but they have been made to be broken. A classical Japanese haiku—*generally*

1. Consists of seventeen Japanese syllables, which are character sounds unlike English, in groups of five, seven, and five. About one haiku in twenty-five does not have a strict five-seven-five form. The variation is seldom more than one syllable in the original Japanese. (Translations leave a lot to be desired.)

2. Contains at least some reference to nature (other than human nature)

> Oh! Don't swat the fly.
> Look at it wring hands and feet,
> Begging for its life.
>
> [Issa]

Most haiku contain "season words" which are direct or oblique references to the time of year, like cherry blossoms for spring or "a bell ringing clearly" for winter.

> Hateful, ugly crow,
> This morning you are handsome—
> Black against the snow.
>
> [Bashō]

Customarily, a haiku poet's work is arranged according to the four seasons.

3. Refers to a *particular* event that is happening *now*, not in the past. The description of circumstances, if it is clearly stated or implied, conveys an emotion. Therefore, the cooperative reader experiences an emotion with the poet. (Editorial comment in last lines, like "it makes me feel sad" violates the imposed subtlety. In this respect many teachers and children go astray.)

> *Baby's Hands*
> One chestnut, only one,
> Is all that he can hold.
> My tiny baby son.

[1] Harold G. Henderson, *Haiku in English.*

Part Three: POETRY

Used properly, these restrictions eliminate unnecessary words. The poet has to rely upon suggestion to record "a moment of emotion in which human nature is somehow linked to all nature."[2] This philosophy is perhaps the most important aspect to American poets,[3] who adapt the other rules discretely, rebelling mainly against the number of syllables and the inclusion of season words. One of my favorite haiku by an American is:

> She wears a necklace
> Of the blocks she passed alone
> After we turned our backs.
>
> [Larry G., age 20]

Haiku stimulate an awareness not only of nature, but also of the importance of words. It is impossible to be verbose. Fake emotions cannot be disguised. For these reasons, haiku are very valuable in the classroom.

Beautiful books on haiku abound. Two by Richard Lewis, *In a Spring Garden* and *The Moment of Wonder*, are exceptional. The translations seem natural and the illustrations for the former book are bold, breaking away from the tradition of Japanese prints typified by the latter. Ezra Jack Keats says of his own painting: "Because of the universality and timelessness of haiku poetry, I chose to illustrate this collection with imagery and style familiar to my own world." *Cricket Songs* by Harry Behn is widely used by teachers. Its selection is very good, but the translator seems to force the lines into five-seven-five patterns with unnatural breaks for English syntax, a bad precedent for teachers. *I See the Winds* by Kazue Mizamura, is particularly good for small children, because the poems capture the spirit rather than the mere form of haiku. The subjects and the colored wash drawings correspond to life in America.

LIMERICKS

Most haiku are serious, at least very earnest. (On the other hand, senryû with a form like haiku are ironic, bawdy, blunt.) Limericks are quite the opposite of haiku—funny and often outrageous. Many collections of limericks contain bawdy verse unacceptable for use in the classroom. As always, it is wise to read the books before showing them to children.

---

[2] Henderson, *Haiku in English*, p. 9.

[3] There is one periodical devoted entirely to haiku: *American Haiku*, P.O. Box 73, Platteville, Wisconsin.

LIMERICKS

Note their rhyme scheme and rhythm:

(1) There was a young man who was bitten
    By twenty-two cats and a kitten.
        Sighed he, ''It is clear
        My finish is near--
    No matter, I'll die like a Briton!''

(2) There was a princess of Bengal,
    Whose mouth was exceedingly small.
        Said she, ''It would be
        More easy for me
    To do without eating at all!''

(3) There once was a boy of Bagdad,
    An inquisitive sort of a lad.
        He said, ''I will see
        If a sting has a bee.''
    And he very soon found that it had!

Finish these:

(1) An otter who sat in a breeze
    Had a terrible craving to sneeze.
        He threw back his head,
        Shut his eyes, but instead

    _____

(2) There once was a fat girl named Mabel
    Who gobbled much food at the table.
        She's clean up her platter,
        Grow fatter and fatter

    _____

Try these if you are having difficulty getting started:

(1) A curly-haired boy with flat feet . . .
(2) A funny old man with a mule . . .
(3) There were twenty-five fish in a school . . .
(4) A sly boy once said with a grin . . .

Limericks introduce the class to conventional notations for rhyme scheme and rhythms. Playing around with the ditto[4] given them for a starter, the children look for patterns and learn to use the alphabet for end rhymes and to keep track of the beat with accent marks.

Ballads and parodies are natural extensions of this assignment. Many of the children are frustrated song writers. Five boys in my class frequently wrote new lyrics to old tunes or pop hits. Nothing was sacred. They did take-offs on take-offs. One boy completely rewrote a Beatle number:

Sung to "HELP!"

Help! I need some candy.
Help! Not just any candy.
Help! Ya' know I need some candy—
   C-A-N-D-Y

When I was young, long ago,
Much younger in each way—yay-yay,
I didn't need so much candy every day.
And now those days are gone,
I'm fatter than before,
And I need more candy
To give me canker sores.

Help me get some candy down-n tow-ow-nn
And I will appreciate it, being round.
Help me get some candy, 'bout a pound.
Won't you please, please get can-dy,
   candy, candy-y.

                        [Cameron M., age 11]

Nonsense does not make doggerel out of other poetry. In general it is cathartic. Children seem to be able to shift gears readily. They can be profound or whimsical. It is a wise idea to give children a variety of experiences in poetry, so that they do not get in a rut.

---

[4] This exercise was in part suggested by a recent sixth-grade text in English for California. The examples are found in a paperback called *A Nonsense Anthology* by Carolyn Wells.

chapter thirteen

SENSES

In high school we used to have a newspaper column called "Pet Peeves and Passions." At that critical and somewhat cynical age of adolescence, we damned the paper—but we enjoyed contributing our ideas to the one column. If they are relaxed and unthreatened, younger children respond as readily to questions which ask their opinions. Part of the section on prose was devoted to this notion. I would like to pick up a thread from there and unwind it a bit further for poetry.

Sometimes children notice unusual details and jot them down. Often they lose interest after that point, abandoning their ideas before putting them into poetic statement. The loss is a shame. The most a teacher can do is openly appreciate the thought and secretly hope that the child may be moved to go further next time. In this chapter I have included some of this raw material, along with the finished work. For practice, the reader can decide which is which. (I'll never tell. The answers are subjective and open-ended.)

Of all the senses, sight is the one most used in the classroom—for creative as well as for mundane experiences. Yet people do not really see enough. Children grow accustomed to their surroundings. They have to work to see more in the usual fare. Rather than make an issue of "using their eyes" in our dark cell of a room, I take the class over to the neighboring park. Beforehand they are armed with pencils and five-by-eight-inch filecards (where there are no desks, these are easier to handle than regular lined paper). They are also loaded with the assignment to look around and write about "Something Only I Saw." If the "only" is not strictly correct, no harm results. However, the children try very hard to be original.

When I take a group of small children to the park, I ask them to do the same thing without the paperwork. They keep their thoughts secret from each other and whisper their observations only to me, taking dictation. The little ones love the mystery of secrets, which we later share back in the room. They snuggle up, cup their hands and giggle their ideas to the teacher. After a child, older or younger, has finished, he can play quietly in the park within a prescribed area. It is nice to have an aide along for an extra pair of eyes to watch the children. Here are a few of their secrets: "Crate [sic] paper on the ground from the Fourth of July." "A boy messing up a girl's hair. They were sitting on the bench there and now the girl is combing their hair. They're putting their hands together." "A thumb tack in the table near a barbecue." "There's a funny tablecloth with pictures on it, knights in armor." "There's a bird under a car, that white station wagon. Maybe it's trying to read the license plates."

Variations on the theme for other short trips could be: (1) "I Am a Camera." The children decide whether they are still cameras which describe one scene thoroughly or movie cameras which capture eight or sixteen quick frames, depicting a continuous action. (2) "The Listening Walk," based on a book by Paul Showers.[1] Younger children could use the book after a stroll to summarize real sounds that they have heard. Older children might want to try out their portable tape-recorders to help their ears.

Questions like "What is the quietest (or the noisiest) sound you know?" or "What do you hear in the conch shell?" provoke observations which are the basis for poetry. So do some paper-and-pencil activities. One such device is quick and effective: each child places five dots on a white sheet of paper. He then trades the dotted sheet with his neighbor and completes

---

[1] Paul Showers, *The Listening Walk.*

the picture. The humorous drawings by the class evoke imaginative descriptions and sometimes poetic statements.

Up to this point, I have not really said much about the relationship of art and poetry. Once I get started on the topic, it is difficult to stop. I feel very strongly that the visual and the verbal strengthen each other. If a teacher can get a child going in art, he will respond eventually in words. Creative effort in any realm opens doors to other media.

Last fall I was particularly pleased with an assignment which started out as an art project. Each child had twelve pieces of 8½ inch x 11 inch paper, one folder, and one week to experiment with texture. He could use any material—tempera, watercolor, chalk, pen, crayon—in his quest to create a variety of textures. The children used all of these, plus fingers, brushes, leaves, straws, spinning tops. The results were spectacular. Each child posted his favorite picture out of the dozen on the bulletin board. These "feelies" aroused so much attention that I asked the children to write a poem or description of at least one of them, not necessarily their own. They tacked up their verbal responses to the visual stimuli. The poems were equally stunning. Unfortunately I did not get copies of them. My wise colleague snapped a photograph of her favorite texture and corresponding poem, so I am able to include her preferred pair. The picture is part of this book's cover and the poem is printed here.

> Amoeba sulking
> Algae hulking
> Duckweed bulking
> Predators lurking
> Satisfied smirking
> And with a sigh
> Remove your eye
> from the microscope.
>
> [Rod J., age 11]

To bring the other senses into play, an indoor assignment like "What do you like to taste (or feel) best?" works fine. Surprisingly, even sixth-grade boys are very earnest about the question. If they have dark thoughts, they never show any. (I wouldn't ask junior-high boys without expecting a repeat performance of *Up the Down Staircase*, where Sylvia Barrett writes the first line of a poem from Emily Dickinson.) Boys certainly seem to respond to tactile qualities more than girls do. At least, the males admit their sensual preferences. The females never got beyond cat's fur, the sun, and snow. The boys wrote enthusiastically:

> The smooth, slippery cowhide
> On the outside of a brand new baseball.
>
> [John M., age 11]

> I like to feel a skateboard
> Vibrating 'neath my feet
> To feel the pulsating concrete
> As I move along the street.
>
> [Charles J., age 11]

> I like to hear the hiss of a snake
> or the roar of a racing car.
>
> I like to feel a smooth gun barrel,
> mud between my toes,
> or snow in my face.
>
> I like the smell of fresh trout
> frying in greasy butter,
> the smell of burning wood.
>
> [Ricky L., age 11]

> I like shishkabob,
> that warm flavor
> running over my tongue.
>
> [Jason C., age 10]

If they ever had it at all, it is this kind of awareness that boys often lose as they become men. Through a different medium, that of dance, Anne Lief Barlin has worked to keep this tactile feeling alive. The boys respond to her unsissy approach and many of them reach a level of expression through their bodies which transfers to the pencil-holding hand. (One of the best dancers in our class was a boy who could not communicate in traditional verbal terms. He is a talented artist who gained enough confidence to share his perceptive ideas in class discussions. He learned to read with the help of special teachers. *Playboy* and *Mad* magazines also played a large role by giving him the incentive. For people who are not fortunate to live in Claremont with the Barlins, there is a handsome film called "Learning Through Movement,"[2] produced by her husband Paul. They also offer *Dance-A-Story* records and books,[3] for preschool to intermediate children.

[2] Available on request from Anne and Paul Barlin, 191 Green Street, Claremont, California 91711.

[3] Anne and Paul Barlin, *Dance-A-Story* series, R.C.A.-Victor and Ginn and Co., 1966. Titles: *Little Duck, Noah's Ark, Magic Mountain, Balloons, Brace Hunter, Flappy and Floppy, Toy Tree, Beach.*

Part Three: POETRY

chapter fourteen

BOOKS

JOURNALS

As I indicated earlier, I am a great believer in diaries of various kinds. The only one of concern in this section is the poetry journal. The children were asked to write a poem a day for two weeks. They were given time in class to ponder and compose.

Their assignment happily coincided with a contest sponsored by the *Scientific American*, which gave them some food for thought. Here is a synopsis of the rules of the game. (It hardly does justice to the exciting advertising in the *Scientific American* and *The New Yorker*:

"Some weeks ago, noting the similarity between the classical paper airplane delta wing model, circa 1920, and the supersonic SST airplane designs, *S.A.* launched the first formal inquiry into paper airplane design.

"We felt that if paper airplane designers were doing, four decades ago, what commercial designers have just got around to, then we should learn if

123

SCIENTIFIC AMERICAN'S
1st INTERNATIONAL
PAPER AIRPLANE COMPETITION

! ! WINNERS IN FOUR CATEGORIES ! !

At Sycamore each class will have its own contest. Choose from the four categories named.

a. Duration aloft

b. Distance flown

c. Aerobatics

d. Origami

JUDGING

All entries will be flown down the Scientific American's Madison Avenue headquarters. The longest hallway is 80 feet, the highest 12 feet, and the widest 10 feet.

Judges will sail the planes down the hall and time flights with a stop watch.

By looking at the littered floor it should be apparent which plane flew the farthest.

Planes still in the running will be tested at the Princeton Wind Tunnel.

PRIZE

The Leonardo, in honor of Leonardo da Vinci, the patron Saint of Paper Airplanes.

(Silver Leonardo to winners not in the airplane industry.)

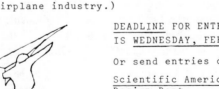

DEADLINE FOR ENTRIES AT SYCAMORE IS WEDNESDAY, FEB. 1, 3 p.m.

Or send entries directly to:

Scientific American Airplane Design Dept.
415 Madison Ave.
New York, N.Y. 10017

Postmarked by Valentine's Day, Feb. 14, 1967

The Leonardo

there's not by now, darting and swooping and gliding its way through the hallways of America, the SST of the year 2,000."[1])

For one week the children in our classroom lived paper airplanes. (They also learned origami—Japanese paper folding. The project became their art, science, physical education, and language programs. Their enthusiasm spread to the rest of the school. The children made many individual discoveries, yet they thought the whole thing was a boondoggle—all play and no work. They were really grateful for the opportunity and the situation never got out of hand. Even if it had gotten unruly, I would consider the venture worthwhile. In the journals I found some poems inspired by origami, the fourth category in the airplane contest. Here is a selection from the children's composition books:

The Origami Seal

The seal sits
all folded up
looking
at you
with a bird
on his head
and he smiles,
his folded smile.

[Beth B., age 10]

Before the Storm

Before the storm
When all is cool,
A sort of different world,
All is quiet,
All is still,
But the uneasiness in the air.
I love the moments,
The waiting moments,
The thinking moments,
Before the howl
Of the gale,
Before the ghosts
Of the clouds
Start the dance.
I love it
Before the storm.

[Holly B., age 11]

---

[1] David C. Hazen, "If we knew what it was we would learn, it just wouldn't be research, would it?" *The New Yorker*, January 14, 1967, pp. 46-47.

Origami

Origami is folding,
making penguins,
making ducks,
Origami is folding
things to life.

[John K., age 10]

Airbirds

The airbirds
were flying
around mountains and hill
and they never stopped
and they never will.

[Susan P., age 10]

Mountain Secrets

The mountains are big
with wondering secrets,
little brooks wandering
and leading to a place
where only the biggest mountain knows.

A bug is barely noticeable
hidden on a leaf.

The mountains can be looked over
from top to bottom
but still keep their secrets.

[Diane S., age 11]

The children did not win any prizes for paper planes, but they did walk off with the local poetry contest. The judges, resident poets and professors, had to increase the number of prizes to accommodate the new quality. Eight schools submitted 350 entries. Five of the six prizes went to our class; the sixth prize went to a girl in the room next door. The poems by the first two girls shared first prize. The other three children received honorable mention.

COMMONPLACE BOOKS

"Commonplace books" are a pleasure to keep and a joy to read. I started one about a year ago, and already it is filled with memorable quotations by famous writers and young children, special poems by favorite poets, including relatives and students, and thoughts that have occurred to me. This conglomeration, a composite of me, is recorded in a blank book designed by Gwen Frostic of Michigan. The pages have subtle etchings in the corners, scenes from nature. The total effect of her work reminds one of Japanese stationery.

Commonplace books are perfect for school. Children can make their own books. Throughout the year they can enter their best poems and thoughts, as well as quotations from books they have read or people they have heard. At the end of the school year, each child has a unique possession.

BOOKBINDING

Bookbinding makes the product of a personal subject even more intimate. Even amateur efforts are certainly more handsome than composition notebooks or hastily stapled pages. There are many good books on the subject.[2] Here I suggest two methods, both very much simplified—a standard book with sheets folded and sewn at the center and a Japanese accordion-style book. These are only two of many possibilities, and may not be the best. But the children can attempt them successfully and, best of all, they are very inexpensive.

Before a book can be bound by any method, it must be written and planned for length and size. The number of pages must be known; it is best, indeed, to make a dummy with illustrations sketched in place and rough-draft reading matter measured or even written around them. (The dummy need not be bound; the pages, with reading matter or pictures on both sides, can be pinned or stapled together.) The process sounds tedious, but it saves time in the long run. The necessity for knowing the exact number of pages needed, including end sheets, will appear as the undertaking progresses.

BINDING A STANDARD BOOK
Description

A book with pages and cover that hinge at the center line, the pages being formed by folding sheets twice the page size. The pages are assem-

[2] Pauline Johnson, *Creative Bookbinding.* Spencer Moseley, Pauline Johnson, and Hazel Koenig, *Crafts Design.*

bled and sewn into one bunch. (It is unlikely that a child will make a book that requires pages to be assembled in two or more bunches.) The end pages are pasted to the cover to hold the book in it.

Materials needed:

Writing paper: sheets at least twice the size of the intended pages; one sheet for each four pages, plus additional sheets to make up for spoiled sheets.

Cardboard for covers: two pieces, each at least an inch longer and wider than the intended pages; these will be cut to the exact size needed.

Heavy paper (oatmeal or construction) or fabric for covering the cardboard: two pieces, each about four inches longer than the intended pages.

Needle and thread (try to get a coarse thread that will not cut the paper).

Glue (satisfactory) or rubber cement (better).

2-inch colored adhesive tape (Mystic or other cloth-base type): you will use a piece three or four inches longer than the height of the intended pages.

Procedure for making the book:

The teacher (*Safety!*) had best take care of step 1 below; steps 2-5 are to be done by the children.

Step 1. Using a paper cutter, cut the writing paper accurately to double the page size, so that each sheet may be folded at the center to make four sides or pages. (Leave the folding for the child.) Cut enough sheets to allow for a title page, a table of contents, perhaps a dedication, perhaps a foreword, and—most important, end sheets at the front and back of the book which will be glued to the cover cardboard. (A work-saving suggestion: You may be able to use paper in a size which the supply cupboard carries. A sheet of business letter paper is 8½ in. by 11 in.; folded it makes four pages 5½ in. by 8½ in. A sheet of legal-size paper may be 8½ in. by 14 in.; folded, it makes four pages 7 in. by 8½ in. You can even use construction paper, usually 12 in. by 18 in., and fold it to make four pages 9 in. by 12 in.; or, with one cut, eight pages 6 in. by 9 in.)

Step 2. Fold each sheet along the center line, as accurately as possible; then slip the folded sheets within one another. The fold locates the center seam for sewing when the time comes to assemble the book. Until then, a paper clip will hold the sheets in sequence. (As extra precaution, I advise the child to number each page lightly in pencil; then if he must recopy or must shuffle pages for any reason, he probably won't lose his place.)

Step 3. Lightly, in pencil, copy onto the numbered pages whatever belongs on them: title page, contents, prose work, poetry, or whatever. Leave space for the illustrations. Ask the teacher to proofread this pencil copy and to indicate corrections.

Step 4. Make the corrections. Then go over the corrected copy with a felt-tip pen and also fill in the illustrations.

Step 5. Check to make sure everything is in place and complete. If it is, then sew the book together down the center fold. Use long stitches, double strands of thread, and backstitch to make a strong book. The book is now ready to be put between covers.

Procedure for making the cover:

Step 6 (*Safety!*) is for the teacher; steps 7-9 are for the children.

Step 6. Cut two pieces of cardboard for the cover; make them the same size, about an inch longer and a half inch wider than the pages of the book. Take care to have the corners accurately right angled.

Step 7. Cut two pieces of heavy paper or fabric for the covering; these should be about four inches longer and wider than the cardboards. (Oatmeal paper does not crack or wear as badly as construction paper.)

Step 8. Center the cardboard on the pieces of cover paper or cloth and mark the paper or cloth to locate the edges or corners. About two inches of cover material should stick out on all sides. Now spread glue or rubber cement all over one side of the board and stick it against the marked place on the cover material; turn over, and smooth out any bubbles. You then have something like this:

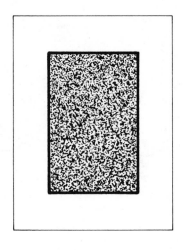

Step 9. Now the bookbinder must fold the edges of cover material over the inside of the board and glue them down. Keeping the corners neat requires care. There are several ways to do so.

A simple method is to cut off each corner of the çover material diagonally, then fold the sides over and glue down. This method has the disadvantage that glue or cement can come through the joint between the edges, but it can be cleaned off and it won't show too much anyway. The joint will be neat even if the diagonal is not cut exactly at 45 degrees to the edges of the cardboard.

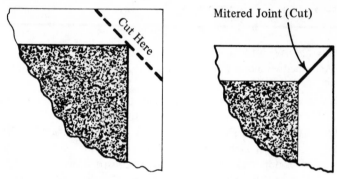

Mitered Joint (Cut)

An uncut joint, a little more bulky, is made by folding the cover material along the diagonal line, then folding the sides over and gluing down. This joint has the disadvantage of being thick (three layers of cover material), but it covers the cardboard, is not likely to let glue seep through, and doesn't ravel if cloth is the cover material.

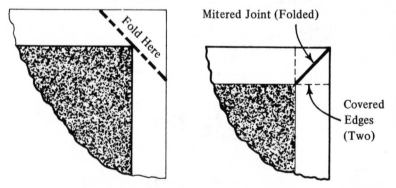

Mitered Joint (Folded)

Covered Edges (Two)

Let the covered cardboards dry after they have been glued up. Keep them flat while they dry by laying a board or other weight on them.

Procedure for assembling the book and cover:

Step 10. Lay the sewn book between the covers, press somewhat firmly, and note the thickness of the book—that is, the distance between the covers.

Step 11. Mark a space a little wider than this thickness down the center of the sticky side of the adhesive tape. Also make marks across the tape to center the cardboard lengthwise. Then stick the cardboards to the tape,

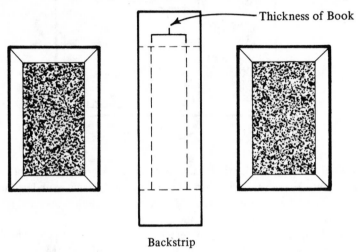

Thickness of Book

Backstrip

fold the ends of the tape over the ends of the boards, and stick the ends down. You now have the cover of the book completed with the tape back strip.

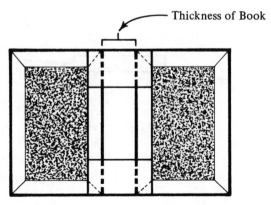

Thickness of Book

14. Books   131

Step 12. Lay the sewn book against the inside of the open cover. Center it top to bottom and line up the sewn center on the inside edge of the cardboard. Mark the places where the top and bottom edges should go.

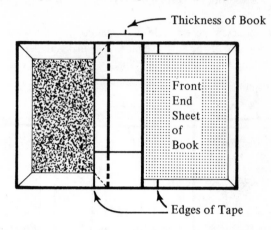

Step 13. Spread glue or cement over the *back* end page and press the book onto the cover at the marked places, with the sewn seam lined up on the cardboard edge. Smooth the end page down onto the cover and leave it in place for a few minutes to let the glue take hold.

Step 14. Now spread glue or cement on the front end page. Then fold the cover over it, taking care to make the corners of the cover line up, and press the cover very firmly onto the end page. Open the book and smooth down the end page before the glue sets.

Step 15. Let the assembled book dry flat under a board or other weight. Several days may be needed.

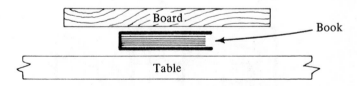

Step 16. Decorate the front cover to finish the book. Take care not to spoil it at this late point. Plan the design on a sheet of paper that is the right size, then use pencil to sketch it lightly on the cover itself. Check for accuracy—spelling for instance. Then finish the title and design with pen or paint.

Except for decoration, size sometimes, and color, each child's book looks pretty much like his classmates'. The pride of authorship and publishing prevails nonetheless. Once the student has gotten the knack of bookbinding, he can experiment on his own with the procedure—perhaps deckle the edges or indent the pages. It is a good idea to leave an empty shelf or bookrack for volumes published throughout the year. Some children become so sophisticated or involved that they design their own publisher's imprints.

The next type of binding is not really harder, although it is stranger. However, to simplify matters I standardized the size. Everybody's book looked basically the same; novelty of style was the distinguishing factor.

BINDING A JAPANESE ACCORDION BOOK

Description:

A book with a continuous strip of pleated pages that opens up like an accordion. The "pages" or section are doubled sheets. The pages are read from left to right along one side of the strip; then the reader flips over to the other side and continues reading from his left toward his right. The possibilities of this format are exciting. Illustrations or headings can extend over several pages, as on a scroll painting, rather than being limited to single pages. The book is hard to visualize without a model, although a

sketch may help; even so the teacher will do well to make an example or to buy one at a stationery store or book shop that sells Japanese articles.

Materials needed:

Cardboard for covers: two pieces, each about 2 inches longer and wider than the intended pages of the book; these will later be cut to the exact size needed.

Heavy paper or cloth for covering the cardboards: two pieces, each about four inches longer and wider than the intended pages.

Glue (satisfactory) or rubber cement (better).

Writing paper: you will need sheets larger than letter size; you may be able to get a roll of white wrapping paper suitable for writing. I use construction paper which comes in sheets 18 in. by 24 in.

Procedure for making the book:

The teacher had best perform Step 1. Steps 2-5 are to be done by the children.

Step 1. Cut the paper into strips, the width of the strip being equal to the height of the intended page: fold each strip into sections of the width of a page. (With my 18 in. by 24 in. paper I make three 6 in. strips and fold each strip into six 4 in. sections to get pages 4 in. wide by 6 in. high. The usual book needs two of these strips; a big one may need four.)

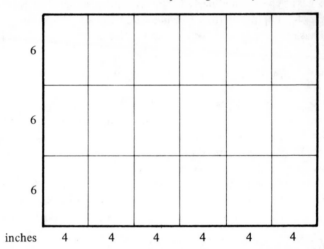

Step 2. Glue two strips back to back with one section extending alone at each end. Take care to have the folds fit together accurately. Apply the glue only to an edge at each end, as indicated in the sketch. This operation

produces two end pages for gluing to the covers and twelve pages for writing or pictures. (By joining two strips end to end and then backing the two double-length strips in the same fashion, one produces two end pages and twenty-four pages for writing or pictures.)

Step 3. Number the pages in sequence (*lightly* in pencil). Begin at the left end of one side of the glued-together strip and go to the end, then flip over and continue to the end of the other side. Cross out the end pages

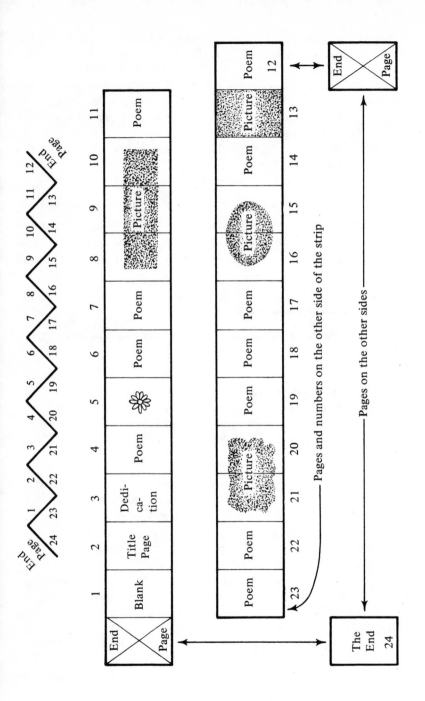

that will be glued down. Note that page 13 will back up page 11 and that page 23 will back up page 1; in the sketch, you are really "reading through" the pages of the back-up strip shown at the bottom.

Step 4. Lightly, in pencil, copy onto the numbered pages whatever belongs on them: title page, contents, prose work, poems, or whatever. Leave space for the pictures. Ask the teacher to proofread this pencil copy and to indicate corrections.

Step 5. Make the corrections. Then go over the corrected copy with a felt-tip pen and also fill in the illustrations. Fold the book together; it is now ready to be put between the covers.

Procedure for making the covers:

Unlike the covers of the standard book, the covers of the accordion book are not fastened together. They can either extend beyond the folded edges of the pages or have their edges even with these edges. Decide which before making the covers.

The teacher (*safety!*) should do Step 6, the cutting of the cardboards; the child can perform the remaining steps of cover making.

Step 6. Cut the cardboards to the exact size desired.

Steps 7 to 9. These are the same as steps 7-9 for making the covers of the standard book, as described above.

Procedure for assembling the book and covers:

Step 10. If the book is to have overlapping covers, lay it against the inside of one cover in the position where you want the book to be. Mark places for the edges or corners with pencil or light pin pricks. Then turn the book over and mark the other cover in the same way. Thus the covers will line up when you paste the book into them. If the covers are not to overlap, this step is unnecessary.

Step 11. Spread glue or cement on the end pages and stick them to the covers in the places you have marked. Smooth the end pages down neatly.

Step 12. Fold the book and put it under a weight or board to dry flat. Several days may be needed.

Step 13. Decorate one or both covers to finish the book.

Part Three: POETRY

OTHER METHODS OF BOOKBINDING

You may find useful suggestions and methods in many books. Some will call for special equipment and will be applicable to bigger books than the standard style explained in this *Ideabook.*

CONCLUSION

This book has been a record of the way one teacher approaches her students and their "lessons." Behind its focus on creativity and writing is the main theme—the education of a teacher or the process of learning to pull meat from the bones of a liberal-arts education and to use it in the daily meals of the classroom.

"Creative writing" has become an overworked and degraded term, implying frivolity, the whim of a teacher who occasionally seeks to excite his students. Invariably, writing thus approached sinks to an effete level—or worse still, to a clerical level rather than being an integral part of life. Teachers, as well as children, need to have a basic commitment to the worth of ideas, and to the necessity and joy of communicating them. In other words, a teacher must *think*. Only then can he set an example by inventing, by weighing the value of his assignments, by trying them out with children, and by showing his students that education is not a finished or closed product. Education must be a living, growing thing. On this premise, he can base a vital program of writing with interrelated subjects, as has been demonstrated in this text.

Thinking is one requisite, reading is another. The teacher must also read to the children, for the children, and for himself. He has and always will have lots of territory to explore—too many books unread. For this book to be successful, the reader must put it down to discover new directions or begin to fill in some of the gaps. Then and only then will the creative process begin for him.

BIBLIOGRAPHY

Adler, Bill. *Love Letters to the Beatles*. G. P. Putnam's Sons, 1964.

Agree, Rose, ed. *How to Eat a Poem and Other Morsels: Food Poems for Children*. Pantheon Books, 1967.

American Haiku. P.O. Box 73, Platteville, Wisconsin.

Applegate, Mauree. *Helping Children Write*. Row Peterson, 1954. This book not only gives the reader excellent ideas for creative writing, but it also boosts his confidence to explore many new avenues.

———. *Easy in English*. Harper & Row, 1960.

Arnold, Arnold. *The Big Book of Tongue Twisters and Double Talk*. Random House, 1964.

Arnstein, Flora. *Children Write Poetry: A Creative Approach*, 2nd ed. Dover Publications, 1967.

Ashton-Warner, Sylvia. *Teacher*. Simon and Schuster, 1963. This book should be on every teacher's shelf for days when the going gets rough. In a natural, engrossing style, Mrs. Ashton-Warner portrays the teacher as a human, who may cry or even dash for a "quick one" when she is moved or tired. There are all kinds of quotable quotes if the reader needs an arsenal for every occasion, like disgusted visitors in a room of havoc, or skeptical administrators evaluating pedagogical performance.

Barlin, Anne, and Paul Barlin. *Dance-a-Story Series*. R.C.A. Victor and Ginn & Company, 1966.

———. *Learning through Movement* (film). S-L Film Productions, 5126 Hartwick Street, Los Angeles, California 90041.

Barnouw, Erik. *The Golden Web*. Oxford University Press, 1968.

Barzun, Jacques. *Teacher in America*. Doubleday (Anchor Book), 1954.

Baskin, Esther, and Leonard Baskin. *Creatures of Darkness*. Little, Brown and Company, 1962.

Beatty, Jerome Jr. *Bob Fulton's Amazing Soda-Pop Stretcher*. W. R. Scott, 1963.

Behn, Harry. *Cricket Songs*. Harcourt, Brace and World, 1964.

Belting, Natalia M. *The Sun Is a Golden Earring*. Holt, Rinehart and Winston, 1962.

———. *The Earth Is on a Fish's Back*. Holt, Rinehart and Winston, 1965.

Blair, Walter. *Tall Tale America*. Coward-McCann, 1944.

Blake, Peter. *God's Own Junkyard*. Holt, Rinehart and Winston, 1964.

Bombaugh, Charles C. *Oddities and Curiosities of Words and Literature*. Dover Publications, 1961. Dover is the leader in publishing works of serendipity because the company deals in reprints of books from by-gone eras when words were bounced around for fun and romance. This paperback has immediate use for the classroom because of its wide variety and universal understanding. The 1961 edition is edited and annotated by Martin Gardner; the original title (1896) was *Gleanings for the Curious*.

Borgmann, Dmitri. *Language on Vacation*. Charles Scribner's Sons, 1965. Mr. Borgmann wrote this book to share his favorite pastime, word games. Its intensity and excitement make me wonder what he does for a vocation. The main use of this book would be to loosen teachers up and stimulate their own involvement in language activities.

Borten, Helen. *Do You Hear What I Hear?* Abelard-Schuman, 1960.

Brown, Margaret Wise. *The Quiet-Noisy Book*. Harper & Row, 1950.

Bruner, Jerome. *On Knowing: Essays for the Left Hand*. Belknap Press of Harvard University Press, 1965.

———. *Toward a Theory of Instruction*. Harvard University Press, 1966.

Buck, Pearl. *The Big Wave*. John Day, 1948.

Cantril, Hadley. *Invasion from Mars: A Study in the Psychology of Panic*. Princeton University Press, 1940.

Carrighar, Sally. *One Day on Beetle Rock*. Alfred A. Knopf, 1944.

Children's Book Council. *The Calendar*, 175 Fifth Avenue, New York, New York 10010.

Clements, H. Millard, B. Robert Tabachnick, and William R. Fielder, *Social Study: Inquiry in Elementary Classrooms*. Bobbs Merrill, 1966.

Clifford, James, ed. *Biography as an Art*. Oxford University Press, 1962.

Cole, Natalie. *Arts in the Classroom*. The John Day Co., 1940.

Cole, William, ed. *The Birds and the Beasts were There*. World Publishing Company, 1963.

Crewes, Frederick C. *The Pooh Perplex*. E. P. Dutton, 1963.

Cummings, E. E. *A Selection of Poems*. Harcourt, Brace and World, 1965.

Cummings, Richard. *101 Hand Puppets: A Guide for Puppeteers of All Ages*. David McKay Company, 1962.

Cunningham, Julia. *Dorp Dead*. Pantheon, 1965.

Dahl, Roald. *Charlie and the Chocolate Factory*. Alfred A. Knopf, 1964.

D'Amico, Victor. *Art for the Family*. Museum of Modern Art, 1954. This paperbound volume is a good, cheap investment for the school and the home, lots of lovely projects which enrich the language art.

Dawson, Mildred A., and others. *Language for Daily Use: Sixth Grade* (fourth edition). California State Series published by Harcourt, Brace and World, 1964.

DeJong, Meindert. *The Wheel on the School*. Harper & Row, 1954.

Douglas, George. *American Book of Days*. H. W. Winston Co., 1948.

Eliot, T. S. "Old Possum's Book of Practical Cats" in *The Complete Poems and Plays: 1909-1950.* Harcourt, Brace and Company, 1952.

Emberly, Ed. *Punch and Judy, a Play for Puppets*. Little, Brown and Co., 1965.

Fenn, Priscilla Neff. *According to Us*. Claremont, Calif. Pi Lambda Theta, 1964.

Fitzhugh, Louise. *Harriet the Spy*. Harper & Row, 1966.

Flaherty, Robert. *Nanook* (film). Athena Film Co., 1922.

Fleming, Ian. *Chitty-Chitty-Bang-Bang*. Random House, 1964.

Franklin, Benjamin. *Ben Franklin's Wit and Wisdom*, illustrated by Joseph Crawhall. Peter Pauper Press, n.d.

George, Jean. *My Side of the Mountain*. E. P. Dutton Co., 1959.

Glubok, Shirley. *Art of the Eskimo*. Harper & Row, 1964.

Hazeltine, Mary. *Anniversaries and Holidays*. Chicago, American Library Association, 1928.

Henderson, Harold G. *Haiku in English*. Japan Society, 1965.

———. *An Introduction to Haiku: An Anthology of Poems and Poets from Bashō to Shiki.* Doubleday and Company, 1958.

Holm, Anne S. *North to Freedom.* Harcourt, Brace and World, 1965.

Howard, Coralie.

Howard, Coralie.*First Book of Short Verse*

Howard, Coralie. *First Book of Short Verse.* Franklin Watts, 1964. Every word of the book is usable in the classroom. Miss Howard has wisely chosen her examples from great poets and great children. A fine review of literature for shaky teachers.

Hutchinson, Ruth, and Ruth Adams. *Every Day's A Holiday.* Harper & Bros., 1951.

Ipcar, Dahlov. *I Love My Anteater.* Alfred A. Knopf, 1964.

Irving, Washington, *The Legend of Sleepy Hollow.*

Jarrell, Randall, *Bat-Poet.* Macmillan Company, 1964.

Johnson, Pauline. *Creative Bookbinding.* University of Washington Press, 1963.

Joslin, Sesyle. *What Do You Say, Dear?* William R. Scott (Young Scott Books), 1958.

Judson, Clara Ingalls. *Benjamin Franklin.* Follett Co., 1957.

Juster, Norman. *The Phantom Tollbooth.* Random House, 1961.

Kaufman, Bel. *Up the Down Staircase.* Prentice-Hall, 1964. For the less earnest moments, the book is fun. The stereotypes do not increase the reader's knowledge of educational philosophy, but they get lots of laughs. It is a handbook of What Not to Do or a thumbnail sketch of an inexperienced Miss Dove or Mrs. Ashton-Warner.

Kennedy, John F. *A Nation of Immigrants.* Harper & Row (Torchbook), 1965.

Kipling, Rudyard. *Just So Stories*, illustrated by Nicholas. Doubleday and Company, 1952.

Krauss, Leonard, ed. *The Autobiography of Benjamin Franklin.* Yale University Press, 1964.

Ladebat, M. P. De. *The Village That Slept.* Coward-McCann, 1965.

Laird, Charlton, and Helene Laird. *The Tree of Language.* World Publishing Co., 1957.

LeCompte, Edward S. *The Dictionary of Last Words.* New York Philosophical Library, 1955.

L'Engle, Madeleine. *Wrinkle in Time.* Farrar, Straus and Giroux, 1962.

Lewis, Richard. *In a Spring Garden.* Dial Press, 1965.

———. *Moment of Wonder.* Dial Press, 1964.

Long, Luman H., ed. *World Almanac and Book of Facts* (annual). Double-day and Co.

Lorenz, Konrad. *King Solomon's Ring.* Thomas Y. Crowell Co., 1952.

MacDougall, Curtis D. *Hoaxes.* Dover Publications, 1958.

MacNeice, Louis. *Astrology.* Doubleday and Company, 1964.

McWhirter, Norris, and Ross McWhirter. *Guinness Book of World Records.* Sterling Publishing Co. (Bantam), 1968.

Meadowcroft, Enid L. *The Story of Benjamin Franklin.* Scholastic Book Services, 1962.

Merriam, Eve. *There Is No Rhyme for Silver.* Atheneum Publishers, 1962.

Milne, A. A. *Pooh Project Book.* E. P. Dutton, 1964.

Mizamura, Kazue. *I See the Winds.* Thomas Y. Crowell Company, 1966.

Moseley, Spencer, Pauline Johnson, and Hazel Koenig. *Crafts Design: An Illustrated Guide.* Wadsworth Publishing Company, 1962.

Muehl, Louise Baker. *My Name Is.* Holiday House, 1959.

Murrell, William. *A History of American Humor*, vol. 1. New York, Whitney Museum, 1933.

Ness, Evaline. *Sam, Bangs, and Moonshine.* Holt, Rinehart and Winston, 1966.

Neville, Emily. *It's Like This, Cat.* Harper & Row, 1963.

The New Yorker. Dec. 4, 1965; March 5, 1966; Jan. 14, 1967.

North, Sterling. *Rascal: A Memoir of a Better Era.* E. P. Dutton & Co., 1963.

O'Dell, Scott. *Island of the Blue Dolphins.* Houghton Mifflin, 1960.

O'Neill, Mary. *Anna Amelia's Apteryx.* Doubleday and Co., 1966.

———. *Hailstones and Halibut Bones.* Doubleday and Co., 1961.

———. *People I'd Like to Keep.* Doubleday and Co., 1964.

———. *Words Words Words.* Doubleday and Co., 1966.

Parker, Don H. *Spelling Word Power Laboratory* (Grades 4-7). Science Research Associates, Chicago, Illinois 60611.

Radford, E., and M. A. Radford. *Encyclopedia of Superstitions.* Hutchinson, 1961.

Rasmussen, Knud. *Beyond the High Hills.* World Publishing Co., 1961.

Reid, Alastair. *Ounce, Dice, Trice.* Atlantic, Little, Brown, 1958.

Richter, Conrad. *The Light in the Forest*, juvenile edition. Alfred A. Knopf, 1966.

Rounds, Glen. *Rain in the Woods and Other Small Matters.* World Publishing Co., 1964.

Sandburg, Carl. *Wind Song.* Harcourt, Brace and World, 1953.

Schlauch, Margaret. *The Gift of Language.* Dover Publications, 1942.

Schoyer, Will. *Schoyer's Vital Anniversaries of the Known World* (annual), Pittsburgh, Will Schoyer and Co.

Selden, George. *The Cricket in Times Square.* Farrar, Straus and Giroux, 1960.

Sendak, Maurice. *Where the Wild Things Are.* Harper & Row, 1963.

Sharp, Margery. *The Rescuers.* Little, Brown and Co., 1959.

Showers, Paul. *The Listening Walk.* Thomas Y. Crowell Co., 1961.

Speare, Elizabeth. *The Witch of Blackbird Pond.* Houghton Mifflin, 1958.

Sperry, Armstrong. *Call It Courage.* Macmillan Co., 1940.

Stanger, Margaret. *That Quail, Robert.* J. B. Lippincott Co., 1966.

Stevens, Wallace. *The Collected Poems of Wallace Stevens.* Alfred A. Knopf, 1955.

Thurber, James. *Fables for Our Time.* Harper & Row, 1940.

Travers, Pamela. *Mary Poppins from A to Z.* Harcourt, Brace, and World, 1962.

Walter, Nina Willis. *Let Them Write Poetry.* Holt, Rinehart and Winston, 1962. This paperback, prepared over a period of years, is loaded with practical hints, extensive bibliography, and large values, as well as excellent examples of poetry written by children. Admirable approach to poetry which ties in with the greater life view.

Weik, Mary. *The Jazz Man.* Atheneum Publishers, 1966.

Welles, Orson. *The War of the Worlds: Invasion from Mars* (record). Audio-Rarities LPA 2355.

Wells, Carolyn. *A Nonsense Anthology.* Dover Publications, 1958.

White, E. B. *Charlotte's Web.* Harper & Row, 1952.

INDEX

Acrostics, 42-44
Alphabet games, 33
Anagrams, 44
Animal crackers, 44
Animals in the classroom, 8-9
Anthologies, 58-61, 104-106
Antonyms, 58
Art work, 74, 120
Astrology, 27

Belting, Natalie, 104-105
Bibliographies, 58
Biography, 13-15
Book reports, 69-75

Bookbinding, 127-137
    standard book, 127-133
    Japanese accordian book, 133-136

Calendars:
    classroom, 50-51
    Japanese cyclical, 28
Capitalization, 35, 54
Cartoons:
    political, 16, 18-19
    Steinberg, 33
Characteristic initials, 44
Charades, 74

Class story, 77-78
Climax, 77
Coatsworth, Elizabeth, 107, 108
Cole, William, 106
Commonplace books, 126-127
Constructed situations, 7-10
Creativity, xi, 2
Critical judgment, 80-87
cummings. e. e., 96-97

Dance, 121-122
Dialogue, 63
Diaries. see Journals
Dictation, 3, 54-55
Dictionaries, 57-58
Discussions, 14-15, 72-73, 76-77
Double meanings, 47-49, 92

Election predictions, 44-46
Equivoques, 47-49
Eskimo art and poetry, 105-106

Fable, 79
"Feedback" assignments, 72-75,
    86-87
Field trips, 7-8, 83-84, 119
Folk tales, 59
Form:
    poetic, 92, 113-117
    prose, 76-79
Franklin, Benjamin, 13, 43
Frost, Robert, 92, 94
Fun, 2

Haiku, 93, 101, 113-115
Handwriting, 2
Heroes: Founding Fathers, 13, 18,
    19, 43
Hidden words, 35-37
Hoaxes, 16-18

Identity questions:
    objects, 25-26
    self, 26-29
Interrelated subjects, 1
Introductory sentences, 62

Jabberwocky, 63
Journalistic conventions, 62-63
Journals, 20, 74, 123-126

Letterwriting, 61-62
Library trip, 83-84
Limericks, 115
Lincoln, Abraham, 18
Literature program, 69-87

Merriam, Eve, 107, 108
Motion poems, 98
Mythology, 78, 104-105

Name games:
    acrostics, 42-44
    anagrams, 44
    election predictions, 44-46
Note taking, 14, 56

O'Neill, Mary, 107-108
Open-ended questions, 22-31
Origami, 125-126
Originality, xi, 99
Outlines, 56

Palindromes, 41
Pantomime, 11
Paragraphing, 2
Penny, 9, 12
Playwriting, 64
Plot 77
Poetry, 91-121
    approach to, 91
Political cartoons, 16, 18-19
Pot-boiler story, 77-78
Praise, 3

Propaganda, 15-16
Prose, 5-65, 91-92
Puppets, 63-65

Questions, 29
Quotation marks:
    dialogue, 63
    puppets, 63-65

Reading aloud, 69-75, 76-77
Reading and comprehension, 86
Role playing, 11

Sandburg, Carl, 92, 94
Science fiction, 78
Senryu, 115
Senses:
    poetry, 118-122
    prose, 23-25
Serendipity, 32-51
Shape poems, 99-100
Short story, 78

Skills, 52-65
Spelling, 53-54
Stevens, Wallace, 95, 100-101
Style, 78
Summaries, 56
Sundry questions, 29
Superstitions, 60-61

Tape recorders, 3
Telephone directory, 9
Television, 3, 20-21, 46, 79
Timelines, 56
Tongue twisters, 33-35
Typewriters, 3

Viewpoint, 11-21

War of the Worlds, 161-168
Washington, George, 18-19
Williams, William Carlos, 95, 96
Word play, 37-41